Higher Education Act
P.L. 89-329
Title II-A

7/15

Feminine
Fulfillment

JEAN GUITTON

de l'Academie Francaise

Feminine
Fulfillment

Translated by

Paul J. Oligny O.F.M.

With Preface by the Most Reverend Bishop
FULTON J. SHEEN, Ph.D., D.D.

Franciscan Herald Press
Chicago, Illinois 60609

FEMININE FULFILLMENT, by Jean Guitton

Translated by Paul J. Oligny O.F.M. from the French work, *Une Femme dans la Maison,* published by Editions du Chalet, Lyon, France.

Library of Congress Catalog Card Number: 65-25841.

Copyright 1965, by Franciscan Herald Press, 1434 West 51st Street, Chicago, Illinois 60609.

Designed by Publication Associates.

Made in the United States of America.

◫◫◫◫◫◫◫◫◫◫◫◫◫◫◫◫◫◫◫◫◫◫◫

IMPRIMI POTEST
  Dominic Limacher O.F.M.
  Minister Provincial

NIHIL OBSTAT
  Lucan Freppert O.F.M.
  Censor Deputatus

IMPRIMATUR
  Most Rev. Cletus F. O'Donnell, D.D.
  Vicar General, Archdiocese of Chicago

July 29, 1965

*Affectionately dedicated
to my sister*

ACKNOWLEDGMENTS

THE translator wishes to express his deep gratitude to the family of Mr. Henri DeMarcellus for their most kind assistance in the translation of this book and for their priceless suggestions.

P. J. O.

Preface

WATERS passing through a valley soon make little channels which, in turn, become deep river beds. The same happens to the stream of thought: it eventually gets into a rut. Philosophy and theology for example, after filtering through one text after another for centuries, harden and congeal into patterns. Then phrases and formulas take the place of thinking. Theology has passed through four periods in the course of Christian history, during which time it became frozen. In the first stage, theology was made by the Bishops of the Church during the first four centuries and became known as Patristic theology. Then, theology was developed by monasteries and became fashioned, to a great extent, after the manner of the lives of the founders. The third stage was reached when theology was developed by the schools and universities and became didactic and scholastic. The fourth, and last stage, came after Trent, when theology was made principally by seminaries and by seminary professors.

In this new era, if theology and philosophy are to take on new life, they will have to pass, like sunlight, through different prisms. One of these prisms will be enlightened theologians and philosophers, but the two new prisms will be the missionaries who will interpret theology in terms of the religious aspirations of the world and the laity who will develop its unchanging principles out of the problems of the modern world.

This book was written by one belonging to the third group: the greatest lay theologian in the Church today: Jean Guitton, a member of the French Academy. Typical of his thought, is his work on unity through love, in which he explored the ecumenical mission of the Church through two prophetic figures, Leibnitz and Newman and revealed new insights of Church as the axis of History. Another treatise of his, "Great Heresies and Church Councils," is a study of Judaism, Gnosticism, Arianism, Islam, Catharism, Protestant Reformation and the Modern mind. Unlike many other lay theologians, he is never negative in his approach. If there is a critique of the Church, it is always the Church to which he belongs. He does not point a finger at the Church as if it were on another planet, or as if the sins of the Church were not also his sins. He is always the loyal son in love with his Mother.

This great mind, which is undoubtedly one of the greatest minds in Christendom, has, in this book opened new doors into the theology and the philosophy of love. Anyone who is tired of reading treatises on love, in which there is an endless repetition of texts from encyclicals, and quotations from scholastic philosophers, will appreciate the profundity and Christian wisdom of these remarkable penetrations into the human heart. Though the book is entitled the "Feminine" it is really more a Niagara of reflections on the outreaching of the heart for happiness. Beginning with the difference of love in a man and in a woman, he writes: "man gives; woman is a gift." Then turning to mothers-in-law, he adds: "if mothers-in-law are sometimes disagreeable, the reason is not because they do not give themselves, but because they give themselves too much." No one possibly could write as well on mothers as Monsieur Guitton has, for he had an exceptional mother who studied irregular Greek verbs in order that she might teach him. "We understand our parents only after their death, and often then it is too late. Every presence is too strong for our gaze, we cannot bear it. It has to be converted into absence before we can enjoy it." The bonds that exist between the child and the mother are closer than any other bonds that exist by choice, because the tension concomitant with choice is done away with, and thought also is done away with. "In the love of a woman you choose to marry, some thought also enters in: you could have chosen someone else. In the case of a mother, we do not will, we acquiesce to a sweet necessity."

Unusual subjects are treated in a fresh way, such as fashion in relationship to a woman; the manner in which confidences are exchanged between lovers, and how they differ from the confidences that are given to a psychiatrist.

The extraordinary value of this book is how it reveals the true "Feminine Mystique." America has been flooded recently with books on this subject, all of which have derived their inspiration from Mme. de Beauvoir, the friend of the existentialist Sartre. The theme of this disappointed woman who finally admits that life and love both cheated her is this: the organic responsibilities of woman must be minimized in order that she may be guided by *custom* and not by *nature*; by *license* and not by *duty*. No one has written so well against the insolence of Mme. de Beauvoir as this French Academician who reminds her that sex, though belonging to woman as well as man, is a temporary situation, and that we are not sexed in the deepest nature of our souls.

Conversation, solitude, attitudes toward the world, all have their depth-soundings; and the effect of time on marriage: "there is also the time when the wife is less beautiful due to habit (beauty is composed partly of surprise), due to her discomforts, and her confinements and also because she feels that she is loved less dearly (beauty is composed in part of the idea that we are loved)." Some of the deeper pages of this great thinker bring out the differences between the early stage of marriage and the latter. Early in marriage, he points out, joy, travel, gifts and celebrations are necessary to weave the cloth of love. Later on, failures, bereavement, bitterness become the cementing forces of union in love. Love, he holds, must be re-purchased daily, by a tender ingenuity. He compares this liturgy, in which there is a beginning again of what is unique and has no possible re-beginning, to the priest who mounts the altar daily to offer a sacrifice that took place only once.

Theologians who are wont to describe the Beatific Vision and the happiness of Heaven, very often leave out the fact that the Heaven also is a City, a Kingdom, a Brotherhood in which there will be the love of one another in God. Monsieur Guitton points out that it is rather difficult for a couple here to understand how they would love each other in God: "I would say that henceforth God plays on our instrument, God alone holds the bow: human beginnings are strictly sonorous chords."

Never does one find one cheap reflection based on Eros, but always the sublimest conception of the dignity of man and a woman and how Mary has become the model of both. Never is there a trite line, a common reflection; never could one finish a sentence that is half-read, so unusual is the thought, so rhythmic the expression. All books on love that treat it from the purely carnal point of view, and identify grace with bodily form, will find from this point on their sublimest inspiration in an author who concludes his work by saying "now I can understand the twofold meaning of the word grace, and why men by a sublime confusion have applied this same word to what is most visible in human beauty, and what is most hidden in God."

One would think that out of the thousands of books which have been written on the subject of woman and on the subject of love, that there was nothing new to be said. But in this new age of a revitalized philosophy and theology, Jean Guitton has come along to change all of those waters into wine.

MOST REV. FULTON J. SHEEN, D.D., PH.D.

Contents

INTRODUCTION

IN reading St. John's account of the multiplication of the loaves, my attention was drawn to a detail which, were it not for my experience as a writer, would have seemed strange to me. Christ commanded his disciples to "gather the fragments that are left over, lest they be wasted" (Jn. 6,12). The account goes on to say that the disciples filled, with the fragments, twelve baskets, the number symbolic of fullness. It is in this sense that Montesquieu said that a book always contains matter for another book. The act of writing calls for severe pruning; the writer must constantly and painfully reject all that would be irrelevant, all that surge of ideas, images and perspectives that do not fit the purpose of the book.

But when night falls, there is no prohibition against following the example of Ruth and, under the moon's crescent, gleaning in one's own field.

The present book is the fallout of my book, *Essay on Human Love*, radioactive dust which I hope will be picked up by some young men and women of our times to help them live this great mystery of love to the fullest in their lifetime.

11 February 1961

Feminine
Fulfillment

1 *The differences between man and woman*

WHILE man is essentially *act,* woman is essentially *nature.* Her intellect does not function like man's. However, woman certainly has the ability to mime; and since our civilization is an entirely masculine one, the woman mimes man's ways of doing things with ease. This does not prevent her mind, were she left to herself, from functioning differently. Instead of analyzing and synthesizing the object, she places herself at a central point, deciding the relationship which the object has to her own life. We express this by saying that she is intuitive and that she understands through the heart. Proofs hold little interest for her and it is very difficult to prove to her that she is wrong.

This process is still more striking in her will. Women do not naturally go from the means to the end. Like Joan of Arc, she jumps straightway to the goal, which she presupposes already attained, and she thinks that once the problem is solved for her, it has likewise vanished for others. That is why women impress men as being stubborn. "What a woman wants, God wants," the proverb says. Just as arguments contrary to her point of view do not embarrass her, neither do failures or refusals sway her greatly. It is possible that the

3

exercise of her senses differs from men's. Touch, especially, keeps her inside an object, as is evident when she handles a baby. In the realm of love, she seeks fusion more than pleasure. In any case she is much more attuned to nature. And that is why (for that restless creature man, who is all *act*) like nature, women are restful.

Women are somewhat *amphibious* creatures who find themselves with two natures and living in two worlds — the most humble material world and the most exalted spiritual world. The woman is naturally made for two things: household and domestic tasks and the exercise of pure love and devotion, and we see her go from one to the other without blinking an eye. On the contrary, man has compartments, sectors, and pigeon-holes in his mind; he likes things to be separate and each in its order. And, although there are sublime exceptions, he is geared for mathematics, for arrangement, for the arts and sciences; he is ill at ease at housekeeping or mysticism, and more so in combining these two opposites. The woman is a mixture, like life which is always double, higher and lower than we think it to be. That is why a woman is ill at ease in the intermediate sphere of "uprightness" and mediocrity. She is a saint or a sinner, an angel or a devil. A drunken woman is much more hideous than a drunken man. Whatever she does, she must *dedicate* herself either to good or to evil. Her situations are states: virgin, wife, mother, widow — yes, even courtesan and "girl." It would never occur to us to apply the same epithets to a man, or at least they would not suffice. And that is why dress, which indicates one's state, is so closely tied in with the woman. She depends more on her manner of dressing. It is the external manifestation of her secret intention, her choices, her elegances. All dress is symbolic.

Man is mind: analyst, dissector, calculator, composer, judge. He has the necessary qualities to be head of a city as well as of the home; but in the latter, as has been frequently remarked, the woman reigns, whereas the man governs. Woman needs a support, a control, a master; but impulse, élan, instinctive foresight of the future, forgetfulness of the past and courage to face the risks of life generally come from her. The act completes the nature, but nature activates the act.

In this way a harmony is effected between the man and the woman. Let us take tranquillity and restlessness as examples and ask ourselves how these two movements of the soul are divided between the two natures. Man, as head, seems steadier than the woman, she being easily shaken by life's jolts. But if we were to probe the depths of man's firmness, we would find that it hides much restlessness, regret and remorse. It is said that man is *strong before the thing,* but *weak before himself* — absent-minded, distracted by the universe. Pessimism, scepticism and the preference for nothingness come from man. Man would be somber and cruel if he followed his thoughts to their logical conclusion. His very works oblige him to seek relaxation. They are dispersed and, as it were, ineffective in themselves despite their brilliance. They need something to unify them, to complete them. The woman is this element who makes amends for time and who redeems it, to use St. Paul's terminology.

It is said that woman is more emotional than man. Is this true? A woman quivers less than man before a sudden explosion. It is worthy of note that women have rarely produced masterpieces that demand a great depth of feeling, such as those of music, painting, poetry, and I will add, philosophy. Mme. de Staël, George Sand, Anna de Noailles and Colette are rich in sentiment and vitality, but delicacy of touch, moderation, nuance of sentiment and keenness of mind must be sought from the minds of men. The woman is much more emotive than impressionable. We know that when a woman gives herself up to passion, she is more ferocious than man. Women are less subject than men to violent emotions such as anger, hatred and remorse. In regard to suffering, they are much less cowardly than soldiers. They bear suffering without complaining; they are not disturbed by the first signs of sickness; they do not give in to sickness so easily. They are accustomed to bear tribulations and pain; it never surprises them, whereas it always does surprise men.

Man *has* a sentiment, a sensation. Woman *is* sentiment, sensation, suffering, love. Man gives; woman is gift. A woman resembles the plant and the flower. Like the vegetable nature, she is serene, sure, deep-rooted, whereas man becomes excited, argues, seeks his prey. As Goethe remarked, the woman resembles water and the earth; man, fire and air. Man is moved to make history, he is eccentric. He represents the act of the era, whereas woman represents the presence of eternity in time. And that is more profound and more true, for time passes and the eternal remains.

At heart the woman is made to transform *truth* into *life* and to make it assimilable. A truth is indeed a marvel. But of what value is it to present a truth if we do not transform it into an assimilable substance?

It seems to me that present-day education leaves itself open to criticism because truths are thrown at children which they cannot assimilate because these truths have not been transformed into the substance of the being. They have not passed through the preparatory melting-pot of a teacher who has changed them into the leaven of life. They have not been sublimated by a person capable of transforming this light into wheat, and the wheat into spiritual milk, as St. Peter says (cf. 1 Pet. 2,2).

This ability to transform the elements into aliments is symbolized in woman when she nurses her newborn baby. That is her charm. Woman's role is that of teacher, because it is through education that one instills knowledge into the very substance of the person. And woman is so eminently endowed in the natural art of making things palatable, of making even bitterness tasty, that she succeeds in making man assimilate the most unpleasant and the most repellent things, even suffering, failure, gradual decline in health, agony, and the death-rattle.

6

2 *Advice to a Girl*

A GIRL must know, recognize and respect the real mystery of the eternal woman in her, whose germ and likeness she carries. The girl of tomorrow, unlike the girl of yesterday, must not be uninstructed, because there is a vast difference between ignorance and innocence.

In this important question concerning the knowledge of life, science is not enough; technique does not suffice. In addition to this, there must be a kind of knowledge of the mystery; and the modern girl seems to me to be one who can both know the laws of life as it is known by the scholar or the biologist and one who will know better than either of them because, instead of making them purely technical laws, she will link them to a mystery which basically is a spiritual mystery.

A girl should have a faculty of ignoring nothing that is, and yet of not allowing herself to depersonalize the laws of life. A girl is capable of this if the education she is given is not only a scientific one, but also a "mysterial" one. The girl needs as her teacher someone who would be as conversant with biology as Pasteur and as versed in poetry as Claudel.

This knowledge of hers must not be restricted to a technical science, but rather should be a total, complete, and full science; a science that does not limit itself to knowing a mechanism, but which knows the finality of the mechanism, that is, its deep significance.

We, say, and rightly so, that science knows facts but does not know the meaning of the facts. Well, I believe that women, by reason of their own needs, will force man to lift himself in some way above himself. He will have to answer the question of the girl who looks at him with deep and searching eyes. Man will be obliged to raise himself up to the science of sciences, that is, to the profound significance of science.

A girl must also cultivate the profound identity within herself, which is not utter independence, but rather unqualified dependence on the source of everything: God.

After my mother's death I found the following sentence among her papers: "More so than man, woman is bound to cultivate her own personality like a sacred fire." Today these words could be given an erroneous meaning. But my mother wrote them around 1905, that is, at a time when the condition of the bourgeois woman was still very conventional. Those were the days when a woman was expected to confine herself to her preserves: currant and raspberry. But my mother had understood (although she knew doubtless how to make preserves) that this was not the principal task of a woman. I observed her withdraw to her silent room, take a notebook, and recopy thoughts which had struck her. In 1912, I saw her learn the Greek declensions so that she could help me review them.

A girl should cultivate her true personality. *She must discover herself and love herself as being different by nature from man, as being different even from her own mother,* because the human species evolves and because the girl of tomorrow must be different from the girl of yesterday.

The woman must live for her children and for her grandchildren, that is to say, for years she will not see. Her duty as woman is to go beyond the present as if she were extended into the future.

To do that, much reflection is needed, because it is in reflecting that one discovers the means of adapting oneself to tomorrow. It is very difficult for a modern girl to develop her personality without losing her femininity. From this point of view, it seems that we have in our tradition a woman who can serve as an example. I refer to Joan of Arc. Joan lived with hardened old soldiers and she highly valued her masculine mode of dress; and yet she bore her femininity to sublime heights! What was the source of her profound femininity? It lay in the fact, I think, that she knew how to withdraw constantly into the depths of herself. That is what is meant by the extraordinary phenomenon of "her voices."

This is the rule of all femininity that wishes to preserve itself intact. And Joan's example shows that this solitude can have the press, the throng, the multitudes as its mainstay. It is possible to obtain atoms of silence, to have time for holy solitude in the subway or at the movies. When all these unknown people, whose destinies we cannot fathom, surround us on all sides, a power of recollection arises. In silent places we are often prone to fruitless reveries, whereas in noise it is sometimes possible to find ourselves again.

The girl who withdraws into the depths of herself will find the secret of being loyally, simply, and purely herself. Then, she will do almost all that man does — but as a woman would do it, in a way that is proper to her and which the man himself needs.

A girl must be ready for the mystery of the future; she must abandon herself to this mystery, whatever it is, by being assured that it will be beautiful, that it will be good, that it will be superior even to her greatest expectation, although it will take on unimaginable forms where suffering will play a profound role.

That is why a girl must assume the attitude of docility, of happy expectation. But she must not seek to predetermine its mode nor its characteristics; she must not give an absolute value to the solution which to her seems the most pleasing or the most desirable. It sometimes happens that girls, having pictured their lives in a certain way, are deeply disturbed if life does not give them the husband or the children they wanted. These disillusioned women go through life with a feeling of disappointment, of resentment against the author of their life. They experience a kind of rage which makes their features morose and which changes them from beautiful to ugly women, whereas if they were homely, they would have become beautiful through the power of acceptance.

There often arises in the course of a woman's life an opportunity to elicit an act of abandonment to the mystery of the future. A girl must prepare a beautiful life for herself, whatever the hypothesis. She must not think that her life has misfired if the opportunity for marriage does not present itself or if she is not blessed with children. The basic vocation of woman, being a vocation of spiritual giving, is a mysterious vocation. It is always possible for a woman, whatever the circumstances, to somehow carry out her destiny which is to bear and to raise up life, spiritual, bodily, or both.

This vocation of life in our civilization has a thousand facets. Motherhood and marriage constitute one of these aspects; it is the most natural. But there are others. A woman must not tell herself that she needs a man to carry out her complete mission. If she wants to, if she is intelligent, she will find fulfillment everywhere and always.

That is why I insisted on the need for a young woman's formation, and on the idea that she must prepare herself for the future. Her vocation can be satisfied in the morning, in the evening, at every moment of the day no matter what she does, because *whatever women do can be done after*

11

the manner of a gift. If the vocation of women lies in the power of her giving of herself, then she must do what she does in a way different from man.

Man acts in an egocentric way. Whatever he does, he brings things from the periphery to the center. I do not say that he is egoistic, because egocentrism does not necessarily have a bad connotation. I even think that a man should not take offense when a woman tells him that he is egoistic; he should answer, "That is my nature."

But the woman acts differently. She is heterocentric. The woman is made for self-giving, and if mothers-in-law are sometimes disagreeable, the reason is not because they do not give themselves, but because they give themselves too much! A woman must know how to limit her capacities of self-giving in order to make herself friendly and respectful of liberty.

In a society where technology is being given an ever greater role and where human relations are being extended to the entire globe, women must play a part to preserve the sense of the human. They must be guardians of the interiority of the family, and at the same time they must open up their homes to others.

A home must have two characteristics. First, it must be intimate, sacral, and mysterious; but it must also resist egocentrism (typically masculine) in order to open itself up to others so that it may truly *be* a home, so that all those who would like to comfort themselves with the light and warmth of its hearth may do so.

Now, for a home to preserve its mystery intact and still welcome others, the woman's vocation of giving is necessary. A woman can be woman in her home by her self-giving. She can create that improbable thing which we call an open home (an extraordinary thing, because a home seems by definition to be closed).

The result of all these considerations is that we expect in the forthcoming years a new type of girl, a type of girl who will be both *old* (that is, one consonant with all human tradition regarding the eternal woman — beginning with Sara, if you wish, and on to Judith, the Sunamitess, Antigone, Electra, and all the Greek and Jewish women — and consequently consonant with eternal femininity, including the medieval and Christian women); and *new*, that is, having that characteristic sign which the end of the twentieth century must seal upon a girl. Femininity old and new must be fused, and we must tell ourselves that humanity must remain faithful to itself by knowing how to preserve the sense of tradition; but we must also realize that tradition is nothing other than progress, because each century had added a nuance, a color, a new and inalienable dimension to the preceding centuries.

The work of mankind here on earth is to develop tradition. Tradition is the progress of yesterday, and progress is the tradition of tomorrow. We tend to set progress against tradition. In truth, they are one and the same thing, and men who believe that they are faithful to tradition by doing exactly what their ancestors did arrest this very tradition.

Inversely, those who think that all that has been done before them must be destroyed and be replaced by something entirely new are men of catastrophe and not men of progress. To develop something, it must be prolonged, but in keeping with its nature. We must then have the sense of logical accretions.

The girl of our times, whatever her nationality, must be a girl replete with knowledge, but a knowledge which is directed toward loving, a knowledge that knows all there is, but knows it in a pure and profound way, a knowledge that penetrates beyond the problems into the mysteries hidden in these problems. She is a girl who will have that gift which the Bible has already pointed out in woman: valor.

Woman (who is pictured as the symbol of weakness and frailty) must also be the symbol of strength. This is how the books of old portray her. Jewish and Greek women are strong women. And the Virgin who sums them up all stands out as the very essence of strength and righteousness.

From this point of view, I believe that the girl of tomorrow will find a strength quite different from the old strength, because it will be blended with knowledge and grace. The girl of tomorrow will be more deeply human. Permit me to quote a text from Raimer Maria Rilke:

"The girl and the woman in their own development will imitate the manias and manners of man for a time only, will ply men's trades for a time only. Once these uncertain periods of transition are over, we will understand that women threw themselves into these (often ridiculous) masquerades only to purify their nature of the deforming influences of the opposite sex. The woman who has within her a more spontaneous, richer, more confident life is certainly more mature and closer to the human than man — that pretentious and impatient creature who is ignorant of the value of what he thinks he loves, because he does not attach as much importance to profound things as the woman does. This humanity which has matured the woman in sufferings and humiliations will see the light of day when the woman has cast off the conventions which condemn her to be 'only a woman.' and the men who do not perceive the advent of this day will be surprised and overcome when it does dawn. Some say (signs already point to it in the Scandinavian countries) the woman will become truly woman. And these words do not only mean that the woman will be the partner of the male, but also that she will be someone of value in her own right, not a mere complement or a limitation, but a *life,* a being involved in history: a woman in her own unique human essence. Such progress will transform the experience of life, today so replete with errors, and that will happen despite man, who may then be out-distanced. Love will no longer be the commerce of a man with a woman, but that of one humanity with another (*von Mensch zu Mensch, nicht mehr von Mann zu Weib*). And this more human love, this love full of respect and of silence, good and clear in all the things it binds and unbinds, is indeed the one that we are preparing for as we battle and toil; it consists in this, that two solitaries protect each other, limit each other and honor each other."

The girl of tomorrow will face the future smiling. She will teach us to look at the future (this future which we always picture under the form of a catastrophe) with reasonable hope, with the idea that the force of love will triumph.

3 *The Marriage of Emmaus*

DURING the fourth year of France's captivity, one of my companions married. The day was Easter Monday, 1944. He had been engaged since 1940. He had the intuition that marriage would be a grace that would enable him to bear and to sublimate separation (for her and for him), by changing this absence into a sacrament. It was, as you may imagine, an unusual marriage ceremony.

It took place in a lamentable hut and with no woman whatsoever present. At the side of the bridegroom was a symbolic chair. At the meal, which was almost nonexistent and which followed the ceremony, I sat to the right of this same empty chair of the wife. It was not a sad occasion, but a rather serious one; a kind of nuptial presence enveloped us. Never had I better understood that the essence of marriage consists in the consent, as St. Augustine said in speaking of the marriage, unique in its kind, of Joseph and Mary.

My friend's marriage took place on an Easter Monday. The breath of the Resurrection was felt even in our world of desolation. This wedding was flooded with the intimate transfiguring light of Easter. I remember having felt, as I listened

16

to the gospel for that day, namely that of the disciples of Emmaus, the connection between the experience of Emmaus and the nuptial aspect of human experience. My diary for the day reads:

"The marriage of Henri G. . . . The story of Emmaus in this nuptial context made me think. Is there a more appropriate page to help us understand the presence of God among us? That particular gospel seems to me to be consistent with what life offers.

"Those conversations with ourselves, full of uncertitude, about the things that concern us most; those doubts concerning the meaning of the great events of this world; that feeling of defeat which even the history of rebirths gives; the irresoluteness of good people; those easy refutations which we attempt to make toward our clearest portents; this need of ours to have a saint as our companion and at the same time our bad manners toward him (analogous to our need to have a saintly spouse and our countless indelicacies toward her). Then the arrival of God in our lives, which comes about in such an imperceptible and in so normal a way — through an unhoped-for meeting, through a commonplace and yet improbable event. Over and above all this, our inability to recognize the presence of Christ *at that very moment* when our heart is filled with him. The meal we shared together on a Sunday night following a walk; the joy of having a friend with us, a brother full of humor and wit, of feeling a support coming from him which we feel ought to be eternal; the surprise of enjoying his fidelity, whereas that very morning we were unaware of it. The day that is *declining,* the night that is coming we know not whence, the fear of separation, of solitude. And then here forever the mystery suddenly appears (and yet so long prepared for), the moment of irruption in a very simple act of breaking bread. Supreme presence in supreme absence.

"The nuptial mystery is also love leaping into hearts with-

17

out one admitting it or even being aware of it, a plenary and furtive moment that may be so quickly shattered. After this, all that remains is a few pieces of bread, duties to perform, a monotonous rhythm, pleasures interwoven with anxieties. But this life will no longer be the same as before. An indefinable memory has been fixed in its center. Every evening meal will revive it.

"Happiness is understood only after it has passed and when it has disappeared: we understand our parents only after their death, and often then it is too late. Every presence is too strong for our gaze; we cannot bear it. It has to be converted into absence before we can enjoy it. Then our memory is liturgical. It is good to enjoy indefinitely what escaped us by the excess of presence.

"This is also one of the aspects of the Paschal mystery. 'It is expedient for you that I depart' (Jn. 16-7).

" 'If I had not absented myself from history, I could not have put myself into the heart of history, and may I add, into your heart also. If I am to live in you through my risen body, I must depart outside of time, outside of your grasp. I will no longer be with you in these conversations along the highway, in those meals, in that temporal commerce that is so motley and so sweet (but where almost everything escapes your restless minds). In brief, I will be more present to you under the bread of the Sacrament where you will know spiritual sweetness in its source.'

"What Emmaus teaches is the radical, nuclear, unspeakable relationship between the highest and the most familiar, that transfiguration of ordinary things by the Risen One, absent and yet more than present. Human life remains as it was. We need do nothing new, only continue what we are doing. Only now all is done in the light of Easter. . . . "

But to return to the story of that strange wedding: I would like to add a word. In the days and weeks that followed that Easter Monday, I happened to talk with the new groom, both

18

of us lonesome, and to ask him with a smile on my face if there was any change in his life. I recall the gist of his answers. He told me that there was a great change; not only because he felt he was in a definite state of life, supported on the rock of the promise, but also because he experienced the presence of two people, a substantial union through the effect of the sacrament of matrimony they had received. Faith alone can make this understandable. Those outside the Faith saw only formality or a friendly illusion.

4 *The Mystery of Marriage*

THE first phase of love is one of initiation, surprise, and mystery. It is a nuptial phase and so to speak sacral, which men do not talk about nor mention in their writings. It is indispensable that the love of man and of woman does not begin haphazardly and in any old way, nor in passion, but that its launching be both visible and secret, an initial, long-awaited moment and something unspeakably solemn that relates the nuptial rite with the rite of death. That is what the wedding ceremony symbolizes, for here joy and seriouness are intertwined in a strange way.

The common idea is that the fullness and perfection of love lasts no longer than a moon-month — hence the "honeymoon." Here we can observe the difference between man and woman which we see already outlined among the more evolved animals: the male partner is more savage, the female more passive, more suffering, less easily excitable to joy. Time, respect, and persuasion are needed to make force acceptable to gentleness. And we already note that this moral is already present at the very outset of love. What is requisite and desirable if the act of union is to be truly an action of unity is

that both parties be not too different and that what is joy for one is not a humiliation for the other. It is clear that this can be realized only with a delicateness that calls for self-mastery, tactfulness, a deep-seated feeling for the other partner, and so many other qualities. In this matter, the vulgar man is devoid of understanding but the spiritual man divines and knows. I borrow from Alain, an unbeliever who wrote so well on love (he belongs to the lineage of Auguste Comte, the tender positivist), a thought that is difficult to express. Here is how his faithful disciple, André Maurois, summarizes it in his book on Alain:

"The animal desire is much inferior to love. If it injects itself into a meeting, it immediately cuts it short and takes away all confidence only to leave room for a very sly and very unpleasant conflict.... The experience of sensual pleasure is dangerous to true love. Yet it overcomes it. We must then compare happiness in love to that of singing with others and of having our voice supported on other voices; this presupposes a marvelous attention. Even in physical emotion brought to its climax by two hands that meet, love is already platonic."

It is believed that the physical unity of the couple is the substantial cause of love. In reality, it is also and above all the effect of the love of souls. We have here a reciprocal cycle where the mind takes precedence over the flesh. And the two are one, which is the wonderful mystery of a love sanctified by oath and by prayer.

This first phase of love is not the same in men as it is in women, a point that men never understand very well and which therefore gives rise to the first rift between the spouses and becomes the first hidden cause of misunderstanding. For man, the life of love does not involve his body, nor has marriage changed his external way of life to any appreciable degree. For the woman, on the contrary, the change is radical and much more so in our civilized societies than in primitive society where the wife remained in the family house. The transformation is both social and physiological. From being a subject and dependent, she becomes a mistress. Furthermore, what was forbidden her now becomes strictly obligatory; what was hardly imaginable is now a duty. And she can no longer chat freely about her experiences with her girl friends.

As soon as she knows that she is pregnant, her being changes. She enters into a cycle of hope and of languor. She does not recognize herself in the mirror. She goes to meet suffering and risk. In days gone by, there was the very real risk of dying young. Man's only way of sharing in this is by sympathy: he contemplates these changes of which he is the source. He feels that he is the cause and is concerned. He is responsible for the one who is coming and consequently also responsible for himself. With these beginnings love is transformed.

The seriousness of life, the thought of a task to accomplish in this world, the expectation of this unknown person whom the child will be, social obligations, the very silence that surrounds you following the social jolity of the wedding, more rigorous control, the masked opposition of the two families — all this adds to the original seriousness of love. Whereas in the first phase love seemed an end, it now seems to become a means to an end which is outside itself: the family to which the man runs the risk of being sacrificed. In the very first phase, we may say that love healed: it was a curative love, a love of the soul. The danger of adolescence lies in solitude, in the impossibility of conquering the complexes of our early childhood, in overcompensating for the failures of life or the humiliations that we suffered from adults. This trouble is dispelled in the life of the couple by the complete community of the first days of married life. Each new day brings a new wonder. The painful monolog of one's childhood becomes henceforth a dialog. What the adolescent found confusing is bound to clear up through telling, through confidence, through the necessity of explaining each facial expression to the other partner. The woman reassures the man by her common sense and her freshness; the man reassures the woman by his knowledge, his decisions in practical matters, and by his richer vocabulary, which enables him to say almost everything. Scrupulous and tense souls, so numerous in our modern society, are comforted by these first days of common life. Moral conscience, instead of being completely internal, reappears under the guise of the person loved; it is then more indulgent. Whatever vague fear our chided childhood left in us is suddenly cured. The word "happiness" takes on a daily meaning, like the bread of prayer.

Surely this mutual supervision of thought and dreams has its inconveniences. It is impossible for differences, for budding quarrels not to arise; but at this early stage what could be divisive is immediately perceived and stayed by the very act of love and by its reproduction, with the result that all serves unity.

Love also enlarges sentiment, for it obliges us to love another family. Generally speaking, however, they are *not* loved. How can you love those who look upon you as a kidnapper, who, notwithstanding good manners, often love you out of a sense of duty, who, despite their protestations of love, welcome you only half-heartedly into their midst, for whom you are not so much a new son or daughter as the possible parent of their grandchild? There is some repulsion where the young husband or wife looks upon the in-laws. Instinct would rather incline you to flee from the parents of the beloved, they being your competitors for your spouse's heart. But love develops here by refraction. If we do not always love our parents-in-law by tender inclination, we respect our spouse's love for those parents and their image in the spouse's eyes. And, by this direct means, while our love for our own parents lessens in intensity, our yielding to the affection of

24

another increases our ability to love.

The child usually enters upon the stage during this first phase of marriage. Here incertitudes are a stronger bond than certitudes. The fact that the man who generated the life does not run the risk of dying because of the birth gives rise to a feeling of gratitude toward his wife. This child, whose character is unknown, for whom we are obliged to have two names in readiness, this two-faced creature who will remain ambiguous until the very last moment — who, however long-awaited he may be, comes as a thief — this newcomer who, although blood of our blood is himself unique, this *child* cannot help but effect a profound change in the love of his parents. His presence will recreate it, will legitimize it, will incarnate it. Before his arrival, the marriage was built on an oath; its substance was fragile, since it was dependent on two wills. At the moment when the life of the couple runs the risk of being spoiled (either because the spouses reach the point where they adore each other or because they begin to stray toward another person), after an almost complete revolution of the stars in their courses, love reappears through the child under the form of a being born of love.

This child, it is true, is but a bundle of needs, a kind of small domestic animal; but that is better for love than if he were already a "thinking reed," because his constant needs, as rhythmic as nature, his frailty, his "non-existence," his sublime aura of distraction that gives him the appearance of an angel, his crises, his mild or serious illnesses — all these constitute a source of common emotion. We know that suffering creates a stronger bond than pleasure. The child is the product of pleasure, certainly, but he is even more the fruit of pain. He obliges love to become even more serious. The child is a third party, but as long as he does not talk (*infans* means "non-speaking"), he does not enter into the society of his parents. Furthermore, he will enter it only later on and always in an imperfect way. However old he is, the love that knitted his parents together will remain a forbidden object for him. The knowledge of the mystery that caused his birth will be concealed from him. No one has ever dared ask his father or mother the story of his conception. His origin is almost as veiled from him as is his agony.

As soon as the child makes its appearance, the future enters — all-fearful and all-hopeful at the same time. And the alternation of these opposite sentiments is so engrossing that, if there is still room for love, it is in a completely different sense. Indeed, as soon as the baby makes one of the spouses a father and the other a mother, he changes everything. Although this latest newcomer is helpless, he now becomes the center and consecrator. In particular, he reunites the husband and wife to their forebears. "Man leaves his father and mother, and clings to his wife," we read in Genesis (2,24). This is true; but as soon as the child appears, both grandparents return and hardly ever leave you. Family unity, always a little divided because of the marriage, is reconstructed around the cradle and we then see the family as an inverted pyramid resting on its point.

There is a danger that the mother-child duo will temper the friendship of the spouses. The duo (especially if it is the duo of a mother and son) seems in its early stages to be even more physical than that which makes "one flesh" of the man and woman. A mother does not have to adapt herself to her child. In the early days the carnal bond between the two is so close that the baby is almost the prolongation of the body of his mother whence he came and which he wounded. Now, at this moment, the child has no physical bond with his father. The father feels no physical relationship between this flesh and his own. Sometimes he wonders at the way the child resembles him, as at some marvel of nature. In other respects the father is a stranger to the child: the father's presence is incomprehensible to his offspring for at the moment he has no need of him. Nothing perhaps better illustrates the

26

idea of the simple and and the sublime than this society formed by the mother and the male child, where opposites are associated in a wonderful way: the masculine form in newborn weakness, and feminine grace (still almost virginal) in maternal form. The father's absence is not felt. He would seem to be a useless protector. The virgin and child form a complete world; God takes up his dwelling there.

But the child, when he is the first one, belongs to one sex only; he cannot express the harmonious dissonances of love. Each spouse must find the sex opposite to his or her own in the child of their love. They must love the sex of the other in an image of themselves. At least the father must have his daughter and the mother her son in order that love leave its fulfilled image.

The first fatherhood, therefore, naturally and necessarily calls for another. The mother forgets the travail of child-birth and remembers only the joy of having given a man to the world. Never satisfied, never sufficient, it is for reasons of health, vocation or finances that the family is limited. Even when the genetic instinct is allayed, a generous attraction impels mankind to propagate the race. In this domain, the law of natural economy is held in check. Affective energy should, by rights, weaken in multiplying, and each child ought to be loved less as another appears. We know this not to ᴏᴇ the case, and with each birth mothers grow young again.

5 The Difficulty of Being
a Mother

MOTHERS! How strangely this word rings, as Goethe said to Eckermann. It is true that there is something mysterious in the very idea of mother.

That life is transmitted through the womb of the woman, imprisoned at first within her under the form of an imperceptible seed which grows solely from her substance; it makes its external appearance in the drama of birth, and for a long time it still needs its mother if it is to live; all this is replete with mystery. Treatises on biology tell us that the nervous system of a baby, unlike that of the great apes, has not reached its full growth; it is only toward the seventh year that the human brain is finally completely formed. The animal is born perfect, the child is still imperfect. Even biologically, the son of man still needs a protective sheath — that is, a mother — in order to attain his human form. This is all the more so in the psychic and moral order where a third of a lifetime is needed to be able to brace the other two-thirds. And the higher our sights, the longer must be the time of childhood and apprenticeship.

In the beginning, the mother alone carries this weight of

life. And that is why, in every city on this earth, mothers are shown deep respect and honored with high praise. We inevitably forget the mother when the fruit of her womb leaves her to live its own life, and more so in the eras where civilization (always so masculine on this technological planet) seems to march along independent and self-sufficient. There are some people who look forward to the time when the mother can be dispensed with and anesthetized. But when they are shown the catastrophic effects of their dream, they return to the maternal arms.

But what is a mother? How ambiguous is this being; how subject in our minds to numerous distortions! Goethe and da Vinci, who gave some thought to this symbol of the mother, did not, to my way of thinking, penetrate to its very essence. They picture mothers in the center of a fluid abyss, majestic and passive like water, images of nature insofar as nature is constantly decomposing, returning to atoms and remaking itself. It is true that the mother is the image of the vital force, the matrix where the human form is fashioned during "the ten months of sickness," *decem fastigia menses,* Vergil said. Or the poets will say that the mother is the image of the creator dream, she who dreams of the future with that look of human hope which Leonardo gives to St. Anne and the Virgin among the waters, the symbols and rocks.

But this is but a very vague idea, and I find that it heralds a temptation. In the mother we honor only power: that (which every woman has) of adding to previous and already old human forms a new form half-made to her image: the child who smiles at her and at whom she smiles, as Vergil said with a sublime ambiguity; the child to whom the parents give a Christian name, the child unique in his kind, who will have his own unique destiny, his history which does not repeat any other history.

To my way of thinking, it is this unheard-of singularity of the new man which is the most hidden mystery in the mother.

THE DIFFICULTY OF BEING A MOTHER

The mother does not only rejoice, forgetting her travail for having brought forth a child into the world, as Christ says in the gospel of St. John (16, 21-22). She shouts for joy because this new man is a unique person, yet an image not dissociated from the father and the mother, in whom the double pyramid of his maternal and paternal ancestors is summed up under a new form. The mother is the person who in her very flesh prepares the human person vowed to eternity.

The mother can be a mother several times. And each maternity, being *incomplete,* obscurely demands another. But number here has no weight. The child is always "unique," in the sense that for the mother he is the universe. And the death of a child, even in a large family, is irreparable. Like Rachel, the mother is inconsolable because there was an unforeseeable, irreplaceable creation in this child who (and this is incomprehensible) had been woven from her very substance. The mother accepts death in order to bring forth her child; that is the greatness of all motherhood: to die and also to give.

But here again, the maternal image can lose its value and become corrupt. And in the mother we can honor goodness in a flimsy, affected, childish and weak way. We may even idolize this maternal love of the earliest days as if, having reached adulthood, it were permissible to become a child again in order to be consoled for bitterness experienced and to have one's revenge on life. (There was a bit of this excess in Marcel Proust's love for his mother.) It is not the intention of the parents that their offspring remain a child, but that from the child a man should sprout with all his strength and all his stature. The mother has her correct image less in the woman kneeling near the cradle than in the erect woman who accepts that her fruit be plucked from her, that he perfect himself in service and sorrow, that he give himself to humanity. That is why the mother is well represented by

31

Mary standing beneath the cross whereon hangs her Son.

We now understand that maternity extends beyond all flesh. There is a spiritual motherhood, even in the flesh, since all motherhood which is not forced presupposes consent, and this is an act of the mind. In our time, when technology offers woman so many means of avoiding pregnancy, the merit of freedom increases. The mother according to the flesh becomes a mother a second time by the spiritual formation she gives.

And how many spiritual motherhoods, especially in our day, are possible outside the family for a girl who is not able to marry or who renounces marriage out of divine love! Married or not, the woman has received a sublime and mysterious power to protect, to increase, to mend life. She watches over its growth. Her mission is to help man to blossom. She gives him the strength to believe and to wait; she is the mother of patience and of faith. The word "heart" describes these two supreme energies since it means both love and courage.

To be a mother. What does it mean, if not to draw the future out of one's being, to create anew, as at the beginning of the world? And even when she does not cooperate directly with creation, for every life that is confided to her the woman is a generator of additional life. In this way every woman is a mother, a mother of the age to come. And, consequently, a mother of peace.

6 *Mother and Child*

MOTHER and child form a perfect and self-sufficient group. And somehow it seems that the sculptor creates and represents this group in a more noble fashion than the painter does. Child and mother issue forth from the same block of stone. At first they were intermingled in the original marble. In the end they become detached, each assuming his and her proper place. The mother recedes a little into the background and the child stands out somewhat; both greet each other with a smile. But with Christmas, the mystery is more profound. The Mother remains standing or kneeling in an attitude of adoration. And the Child is lying in the manger. For the same time the Mother adores this Child who is her God. And he contemplates this Mother of his choice.

The mystery of mother and child seems here to transcend human things, because the Child is God and the Mother is the Virgin; the father figure who protects and shelters like a shadow is not the real Father. At Christmas, we are out of this world and closer to eternal models. And yet it is in this celestial mirror of our condition that we perceive it more purely. For divinity has this about it: it does not destroy the human but rather sublimates it.

In this case, the Mother is truly the mother. In other words, the Child comes from her body and from her consent; and he is born also, like all of us, of the breath of the living God. The Child looks like his Mother. It is true that the children of man are the impress of their mothers of whom they are, as it were, the incarnate idea in the male type and in history. The Child is helpless and completely dependent, the image of man's condition with respect to God. Each day's milk will be given to him on that day.

He does not pray because as yet he is incapable of any distinct thought or speech. But he is in the posture of prayer, lying on the ground, "like the earth, parched, lifeless" (Ps. 62, 2), standing before God in poverty, asking everything, entitled to everything. The Mother, too, sensing her helplessness, wonders how the miracle of the birth and the continuous miracle of nursing came about.

She prays God to sustain her, to deliver her of herself. And already she is delivered, for from now on her center is outside herself, in this Child who represents God on earth.

Then all gather to wonder around the Mother and Child; they lean over this unknown face to see how it is fashioned: this forehead, this gaze, those hands, whether he resembles anyone and, if so, who. Everyone says many things, all of them false and all of them true. Men of every status group around this Child: the elite and the poor, shepherds and kings, wise men and magi. The animals, too, receive a blessing.

The Future is present — the Future, the image of the Eternal. We know nothing. We surmise everything. We are on the point of seeing everything. The prophets unloose their tongues, foretelling joy and suffering, necessary and combined.

The atom is there, which risks destroying everything on this earth. But the Child — even more wondrous, more fragile, even more improbable — is there. He makes his entry into this menaced cosmos. And he smiles.

7   *The Son Contemplates His Mother*

I PICTURE my mother at an age I have long since passed. We cannot make a dead person grow old. He always remains what he was when he died. A widow of World War I said to me: "I can no longer conjure up my husband, who would be the age of my grandson." Those who lost their mother prematurely have the same difficulty.

And yet this equalization of ages is helpful when it comes to a mother. The distance which separates a child from his parents is too great in those early years when we are like tiny animals, toys of flesh for our parents. This relationship is too biological to my way of thinking. Little by little we take on consistency and shape: the strange hiatus is made up. Towards the middle of our life the gap is apparently filled, at least in appearances — especially in our modern age where there are no more old faces nor old women. We then seem to have the same age as our parents; when we accompany them, we seem to belong to the same generation as they do.

Likewise, despite the dates inscribed on tombstones, the dead all seem to us to have the same indefinite age. In this way is prepared that rush of the human race into timelessness.

FEMININE FULFILLMENT

The history of a son and his mother is the history of this slow metamorphosis, from the moment he was a nursling to that age when he went for a walk with his mother at his side and talked to her as to an equal, as to his mysterious, former and dissimilar image, more weighted with years it is true, but also lighter and purer than himself.

Why must man's first discovery of femininity, which will trouble him later on, be under such a peaceful form in the being who carried him, and where, beginning as an imperceptible seed, he silently became her own body, her soul, and her person? We usually study this difference of sex in connection with physical love. But there is no discussion nor scarcely any thought given to those relationships where physical love does not enter: brother and sister, father and daughter — mother and son, that almost sacred couple in Christianity. Here the flesh does not enter into the picture. Sex is only a particular case of a relation of dissimilarity. The remarkable thing about these attachments is that sexuality does not enter into them; they are spiritual loves, although natural and without the aridity of other types of spiritual loves.

And I would also add that there is no choice in these friendships and that is what gives them something divine. We have no choice about being born nor about our parents. And the father and mother had no choice in your peculiarities either. It is a strange thing that a woman can "expect a child," not knowing his sex or his personality, and yet knowing that she will love him. I believe that the bonds which are formed without choice are the strongest, because the tension concommitant with choice is done away with. Thought is done away with. Thought is needed to love a father, because the bond between you and him is not immediate. In the love of the woman you choose to marry, some thought also enters in: you could have chosen someone else. In the case of a mother, we do not will; we acquiese to a sweet necessity.

36

THE SON CONTEMPLATES HIS MOTHER

This does not mean, however, that mother and son have a clearer knowledge of each other. Quite the contrary. The farther back I went into my mother's life, the more impressed I was that I knew nothing about her. I could not picture her as a young wife, much less as a girl. How strange it is, I said to myself, that it is almost forbidden to go back to one's own sources; we verify that law of all knowledge, namely, that everything becomes clouded near its origins. How shrouded will the circumstances of the marriage to which they owe their birth ever remain for children? . . . And even if they knew them, how would they justify those accidents of yesteryear which brought it about that this man and this woman met each other — accidents that were so tenuous, sometimes so fragile or so conventional and which could have been quite otherwise? And yet from this accident, from this chance crossing, I result with all my indestructible substance.

8   *Rites of the Home*

WHAT we have seen done is what educates us. Everything happens as if the period we call youth and even maturity (the period when man works for his social groups and for mankind) was a sort of parenthesis, after which the course of our former life, of our ancestral life, having been momentarily interrupted, begins again. Then the memories of childhood return in a new light; then especially the first habits reappear and with them the incorporated traditions, the heritages.

Michelet, who had observed the men of history, claimed that at the age of fifty, one's individual sickness gave way to hereditary sickness; for example, Louis XIV suffered gallstones and Napoleon from liver trouble. But this is true not only of sickness. The hereditary good appears with its structure when the foliage of life has been carried away by the November wind.

I would like to apply this law to the training received in the home. This may be useful in this age of general scepticism when man "revolts against himself," uproots himself, when he loves to call himself "the son of no one," without father, mother or genealogy, like Melchisedec.

As some view it, there is an inferiority in having lived as a child in an environment permeated with faith. Or, at least, the sign that one has at last become a free spirit is that one has rejected this first acquisition, thanks to virile reflection. The type of story that is always well received in France is modeled after Renan's *Souvenirs:* we forgive a man who believes in God provided he did so early in life, and if as an adult this belief remains in the back of his mind like the vague and sweet persistence of a poetic memory. The faith is judged to be fortunate, fertile, and worthwhile when it envelops the birth of the person in a factitious and maternal atmosphere. It is agreed that it can be helpful in the formative years) it is even noted that those lacking this environment of faith carry about within them a basic dryness and rigor; such persons are poorly in touch with other consciences, with nature and its mystery. That is why a good Hegelian will say that it is proper to begin with the faith, which is the truth of childhood; likewise, to be a man, it is very necessary to be nursed, to be surrounded with warmth and care. Without the love of a mother, without her delicate influence, the cartilages would solidify too soon; one would become a kind of child-man, a monster with no childhood. And this is the shortcoming of some geniuses, for instance, Pascal, Racine and Kierkegaard. These men lost their mothers too early in life. They seem to have been born of a sudden and without preparation.

But man cannot remain a child forever and the problem facing everyone is to escape the excesses of parental love, this provisory innocence, without too much damage, too many crises and ruptures, simply by the insensible effect of growing up. Childhood must terminate in us by an initiation to existence, which respects the first mystery but also abolishes it. . . .

So thinks the modern unbeliever who knows that every belief has its moment of truth, provided it can disappear or rather sublimate itself into a higher idea. The belief of childhood is, as Leon Brunschvicg said, an *"âge de l'intelligence,"* useful to have gone through, but which must be left behind at the age of reason. The unbeliever will always ask himself how Pascal could have declined to pursue his mathematics on the infinite. The unbeliever will never understand how Pascal acquiesed with a free and informed adherence to the certitudes of his youth, reapproving within himself in a higher light the first acts of untried faith.

It should be noted that the kind of certitude possessed by the child is not the same as that of the instructed adult. It is true that a metamorphosis is indispensable. And the difficulty of this metamorphosis is constantly increased in a society in which the environment of the adult is a motley, polymorphous and skeptical environment which is very different from the milieu of the child which is calm, closed and conformist. Is the faith of the child and of simple folk an act deprived of reason, explainable only by the constraints, the influences and the suggestions of adults?

If I consider my own experience, if I attempt, as Newman did, to define "my first religious impressions," what I find are my first impressions of existence. The sense of existing and the sense of the divine were awakened in my soul simultaneously. Modern philosophers speak of *Dasein,* the being-here-and-there. What the discovery of this *Dasein* must be for a child reared in disbelief, I have no idea. To me it seems impossible that the *Dasein* of the child is a *Dasein* "for death." The child does not know death. To feel himself here and there and to believe in God is one and the same act for him, as it was for Descartes.

My first impression of existing was precocious. I still remember it, as a sort of panic. By my "impression of existing" I mean that of being apart in the midst of things, a stranger even to those who love you, of existing for oneself, for oneself alone, a solid and indestructible accident.

In a familial religious formation, this conscious awareness is not distinct from the aids of religion, from its transcendent and familiar images. Religion does not insinuate itself by any will to believe: it is given in the home itself, of which it is the prolongation. It is imbibed with our mother's milk. At the time, it has a different aspect from what it will have later on in adulthood. Even the firmest believer feels the difference between these two universes: one visible, the other impalpable and unexplorable, which surrounds and penetrates the visible invisibly, which is ever the object of an intention, of an élan, of a desire, but never of a sight. And if faith looks for the signs of the Guest in this world, he finds only traces in the sand.

This is not the case in early life. Religion is mingled then with the essential sentiments which will give the personality its structure. Precisely because mothers feel and know these bonds, they elicit acts of faith from the child at the same time as the first impulses of life are forming in him, in order that faith and life may come from the same source. The sensation of living, of being loved and of believing then merge and are one.

Likewise later on when conscience chooses between good and evil, it harks back to a Presence who is pleased or saddened, to a mother-being who smiles or cries over you; and duty is never presented as an obedience to mere rules, as it is in textbooks.

Furthermore, since the very foundations of religion and its laws are inevitably associated with churchly sites, one's religion is associated with a kind of "atmosphere of godliness." This atmosphere is present in city churches, but perhaps even more present in country chapels. The crucifixes and the romanticized statues of the Blessed Mother magnify this earthly Presence because they evoke childlike faith.

This sentiment of a quasi-local Presence also existed in paganism and constituted much of its grandeur; it rooted the gods in nature, which thereby became a sacrament. I am speaking here of true paganism (that of Vergil) whose religion was an exaltation, and not of that false naturalism of the modern where religion has become a degradation.

Just as the pagan child brought up in the religion of the Fathers or of the Lares found the gods everywhere and saw them incorporated in the daily element of life, so too for the Christian child, in families, faith is not only a rite or an acquired dogma but a *religio* (bond) in the strong Latin sense of the word. That is why those who were brought up in this piety, even if they lose a formal faith (as did Goethe) often preserve "religion" as a respect, a mystery, a relationship to a nameless eternal Being.

When I was a child, the divorce introduced by the life and knowledge of men did not exist for me; the distinction between morality and religion would not have made any sense to me. Everything was much more simple and certainly more like what transpired in primitive societies (even though our knowledge of these is meager because the sociologists wish to belittle human origins). In all things, origins are the most obscure, the most tangled; they are the place where the most exalted and the most base meet; but the wisdom of the Church has purified that which was mixed with impurity in the natural rites of the home. Thanks to the Church, we may abandon ourselves to our being.

In a Christian people, there is a possibility that traces of superstition exist; but it is a purified, liberated superstition, assimilated by grace, and used as an instrument, as when a pilgrimage sanctified a sacred pagan forest. The mythical Santa Claus is kept, but as a symbol of a lasting truth: that of God the Giver, friend of the simple of heart, and Giver even more so during the days of night and of snow.

So it is with the rites of the home, of persons and of things. The father, the mother, the little brother, the table, the bread, the bed, the door that opens, the guest who comes,

the primer, the sign of the cross, joined hands, eyes lifted heavenward, guardian angels, hymns, the solemn priest, the enigmatic Mass, the Host on the lips: all this makes up not two worlds, but only one.

The distinction between heaven and earth does not exist, and even less that of immanence and transcendence. It is poetry — it is truth, Goethe would say, for he was unwilling to dissociate these two lights. Many tears or great genius would be needed to rediscover this in old age.

9   *A Woman in the House*

"O WONDROUS friend, what my heart conceives is to possess your goods as the lady of your house, your arm resting on mine." The antiquity of this Egyptian text, "A Song of Love," written several centuries before our era and which the sands have preserved, shows how true these sentiments are. The wife possesses the goods of her master. Her heart is so made that she does not know where the person she loves ends; in her mind he extends even to the walls, to the roof, to the fields, to the milky Nile beyond them, perhaps to the rose-colored pyramids, to the entire sky. Everything belongs to him, since he is loved. Everything, too, is hers, since she is loved. The gods belong to them, too. So do the dead.

On this earth, man and woman, without interference, taste the full joy of being *like* creatures. Pascal said that man cannot bear to be alone in a room and that he prefers cohabitation to solitude.

When we love with an incarnate love, how true it is that things come to life and that we become the proprietors of everything! I am surprised that Adam was able to call all things by their names before his wife was created; but we

must note that this took place at the time when he was about
to fall into that deep sleep from which Eve emerged. When
he named the beasts of the field and the birds of the air, she
was already his. She was the as yet unknown fiancée of his
flesh. And from then on things could have a name in her, in
order to be made subject to, lucid to man.

It is the woman who makes the house, more than the ma-
son or the roofer. I call my own house "my interior," as if it
were the interior of my self rather than its shell. But it is this
shell that enables me to live my secret life: this exterior gives
me an interior. In contrast, there is no "innerness" in a hotel
room. I know that some people prefer such places because
they find the same impersonal walls in every one of them;
they are at home everywhere, since they have no roots; they
are free of everything. But I do not belong to that nomadic
race.

I approve of those stable persons who can live well only
in an interior surrounded by objects which, like pictures of
friends that hang on the wall, seem to look upon you as
their cynosure. Whatever things a woman acquires in her
house, she gives a kind of friendly and protective twist, like
the bird that bends twigs to make a nest. Without the woman, an object remains just an object and not a symbol. Such
emptiness, such an absence of response from things is worse
than nothingness. The echo is missing.

It is the woman who creates a home out of what was formerly a mere dwelling place. Whether it be a house, or an
apartment, or even a tiny studio, it is the woman who takes
care of it more so than the man, because she reigns in the
human home. The household items are the fruit of her
thoughts. Her home is to her a prime work of art executed
with objects and furnishings, to which the woman tries to
give a lilting form, that special character which the bird, as
I said, gives to a formerly lifeless twig. There are so many

difficulties to be resolved before finding the perfect piece of furniture; so many conflicting demands that seem impossible to satisfy! Interior decorating problems sometimes become insoluble. The time may come when they are left unsolved, when the interior of the house stays as it is, when chance and disorder triumph in the end. The house may remain like a mountain or a rock shaped by random forces. And the pictures on the wall still hang over the spots, in a manner long hallowed by custom. But the woman is ever queen, sometimes by reason of her restlessness which impels her to change things, sometimes by her spirit of acquiescence which brings her to say: "Let things stay as they are!"

Yet there are always some changes in a house where the woman reigns. For this restless yet stable creature is so made that she cannot be herself if she does not always appear a different person. A woman in the house transforms. She wants to renew the same old thing, make it somehow different. She would like to give to that simple shelter, the house, the allure of a grotto of enchantment. . . .

She does something similar in adorning her body. I know children whose first idea of the magic beauty of "another world" came when they saw their transformed mother leave for a party, and I believe that Baudelaire was of their number. A woman's dress is a commentary of her own beauty, which she gives to others, showing what in her body can become an object of contemplation. The shape and color of the fabric reveal that beauty, and the small accessories, the pins and clips, the necklaces, the rings, and the other adornments sparkle for a moment like lighthouses on the sea. All this changes with every season: it is the *style*. There you have a profound word that is indicative of what is necessary and magical in the change.

The mystery of fashion is that this sudden change of detail is imposed on women; they cannot escape it. No one creates or really launches a style. Or, if they do launch it, they do so because there is a general agreement, an obscure appeal. In matters of style, women obey some hidden law analogous to the one that decides the colors of the wings of birds or the petals of flowers. She makes clothing, which is of industry, re-enter nature.

Each morning, the woman is there in the home, which seems to smile, to exist, and almost breathe in her. She has arranged everything. She has waged constant war against the encroaching dust. The roaring of the vacuum cleaner stops only to be replaced by the lowing of some unknown mechanical beast, like the siren of a boat in distress. The dust is absorbed, like small concerns should be by a peaceful soul.

In the East as in the West, throughout the world, the woman is there in the home, an image of durability and of permanence in a time which, nevertheless, passes. She struggles heroically against the return of the dust and against disorder. We ask ourselves why she is so concerned: the children will be returning from school; others will muss the brief perfection. The answer is that nature is luxurious, overabundant, shining, and that the house must be made to imitate nature through her superfluous attentions. The superfluous gives presence to things.

And that is why however varied, however entertaining a mountain or an ocean or even a countryside during holidays may be, a secret voice (which we are too proud to acknowledge) murmurs: "Oh! how good it will be to get back home!" In a joke, I read that a home elicits two contradictory pleasures every day: that of getting out of it and that of returning to it. The latter prevails, it seems to me.

10   *Early and Late Marriages*

CERTAIN people reach intellectual maturity very early in life. Evariste Galois did much for mathematics before dying at the age of twenty-one in a duel. And Mozart had discovered everything at sixteen. Others sleep away their childhood; they are like winterbound mountains without vegetation. Then, toward the middle of their life, they awaken. For still others springtime comes in their later years. Elsewhere I have described my old professor, M. Pouget, who belonged to this latter race: after sixty years of silence and of application, his genius blossomed in his eightieth year.

We admire precociousness because of our naive love for wonders: the surprise of that child who knows without having learned how to win us over, and our own astonishment at his precociousness. The "youth" of old people ought to engage our attention more.

In married life, the very young may commit themselves before knowing the pitfalls ahead. Like Goethe or Montherlant, who went straight from college to the excitements of the battlefield, precocious couples risk bungling their destiny by a prolonged adolescence, because they

50

throw themselves into the firing line too soon. Montherlant never recovered from his disillusionment. Goethe was too intelligent to believe that he was marked by the cannonades of Valmy. When death has been too familiar to us, when heroism seems but a game, then it is hard to return to the ordinary pathways of life. Those mathematicians, musicians, even those mystics who made their discoveries too early in life are uneasy, when they grow old, about their early glory. As for those girls who are mothers at eighteen years of age and for whom nursing is a continuation of their childhood games (as was their night of love), I doubt whether they will ever be mature women. They thought that they could sidestep the transition, but the intervening stages take their revenge under the form of a lacuna which in the end becomes permanent.

Another disadvantage and risk of any early engagement is that one is prone to made bad choices that carry one off course. But, on the other hand, what freshness, what buoyancy there is! What persistence in those lives which are stabilized completely around the age of sixteen, and for which there are no regrets. They are the fulfillment of the marriage blessing which foresees young great-grandparents seeing around them the children of their grandchildren. In times past this was not a rare blessing, because strong institutions chose a partner for one, allowing one to make a more suitable choice very early in life. There may have been a struggle for conjugal adjustment, but there was none for material security; the fledglings were welcomed in the old homestead.

The advantage of the late marriage is that we bring more experience to it and thus more joy is derived from it. Before putting a yoke around our necks and restricting ourselves to one single choice, we knew diversity. We remember it; we still breathe it as the harmonic of this definitive choice. Our choice was like a September fruit that finally fell from our fulfilled essence.

Such was the case of the Apostle Peter with his memories of his mother-in-law, his storms at sea, his fishing. It was only natural that all these ordinary human things would find their way into his writings, that they would give him that quality which I inhale in the writings of Mark, his interpreter. And Kant in his old age — he was fifty when he wrote — also betrays in his serious discourses a long meditative authority. It is not rare in present-day America to hear that a man of forty has taken up an entirely new career. I say that the experience of one's first way of life cannot be erased: it strengthens and seeds the rest.

But we must admit that we like to take risks, that there is a spirit of exaltation which accompanies youth and which never returns. The old fossils who try to be exuberant annoy me: the time has passed. The works and loves of later life can be fathomless, can even preserve a certain mysterous youth about them (as in the second *Faust* or the *Satin Slipper* of Claudel); but they lack the glorious awkwardness of innocence.

We can apply these insights in the discernment of religious vocations. I think that it is preferable to encourage souls to enter the religious state early in life, provided the young candidate is not too immature and does not enter before he has gained complete mastery of himself. But it is good that nature and history, governesses of delays, beget belated vocations. We always do everything too soon. And every delay is an educator. There are events, circumstances, delays, and obligations which often oblige a man to do late in life what he should have done in his youth; so it is with belated vocations, as were those of the Apostles.

Basically, the early commitment is man's way. The belated is the method which God has reserved to himself. He, the absolute master of time, is able to wait.

II   *Confidences*

CONFIDENCES are comforting, but we must know how tc choose. A confidant is like a hiding-place where we bury a treasure. A confidant is also a veiled-faced pythoness from whom we expect an oracle. And finally, a confidant is a mirror where we look at ourselves.

Once a secret is shared, the human heart feels glad. But it is rare when this gladness is not immediately followed by a feeling of regret. "I have often bit my tongue for having spoken, but never for having kept silent," said Cardinal Saliège. Yes, we always say *a little too much*: either we exaggerate or we reveal what should not have been said. Yes, even we ourselves can be guilty of this! It is so difficult to be truthful with other men. This is all the more true when we confide in a person and want to show ourselves in a favorable light. And this is again true (paradoxically) when we obscure our case so as not to be altogether understood or so as to lure the other person into agreeing with our confession.

There is a great deal of coquettishness in confidences, barring the rarity of perfect abandonment. And that is why we should restrict our confidences to very few people. They should be people who are, as it were, mothers to us — that is, those who could have borne us and breast-fed us, to whom we reveal nothing that they do not already know or that they could not surmise from our unconscious actions.

To take some still immature, unreliable and inquisitive person for our confidant to whom our confidence will be a revelation of what he did not know, would not be a wise course. If the confession be a confidence of evil, it it should be given only to one placed in a divine and maternal attitude, who knows beforehand "what is in man," someone who is able "to bear the sins of the world." We could not go to confession to a teller of tales — to a Balzac or to a Mauriac. Those who really know man are silent about him. Novelists write exhaustively about one single person: themselves —inflated, justified, transposed, condemned only in appearance, commiting pretty but never debasing sins.

We do not offer genuine confidences on the psychiatrist's couch. We unburden ourselves of an opaque growth. We vomit an indistinct thought, an old memory which we did not know about ourselves. The therapist is not there to hear you as a mother would hear you, but to help you to cast off your mental calculi, to receive them in his cuvette. In fact, he does not really receive these recollections; we might say that he checks them in and signs for them and that he is their "receptacle," which is quite different from being a confidant.

This brings me to the point that friendly confidences demand reciprocity. In the case of a doctor or a psychiatrist, there is no such thing as reciprocation. They do not say to us: "I am a sick man, too." The psychoanalyist makes even less of a confession. He does not say: "I, too, have my troubles." For that matter, even the priest-confessor does not say: "I, likewise, am a sinner." Moreover, we demand that they be impassive, identified with the act of pardon, of knowledge, of health. If they are to cure, they must be lifted outside the human condition. We must see in them the power and no longer the man. If they remind us that they are suffering from the same weakness, they would render a different kind of service, but it is not this kind of service that we are asking of them in these audiences where we come to them as a questing sick person.

The solace in friendly confidences consists not only in what is given by way of a secret but what is received from the other's secret. And then, what a surprise is in store for you! You notice that he suffers from the same evil. That is the beautiful fruit of this twofold confidence: we are tied to it by the complicity of two weaknesses which then make one strength.

12   *Conversation*

WE often learn more in a conversation than we do from reading or from a lecture. And yet the essence of conversation is not to have a subject. But precisely because it is without a subject, it teaches you. To have a subject is to have a goal, and the goal often hinders the stroll. The person who takes a walk with a destination in mind takes an excursion, he is no longer taking a walk. Strolling, sauntering, and conversation have this interesting element about them, that surprise follows surprise. When Socrates let himself go, he taught; when he set a goal, when he allowed his disciples to bleat "yes," "certainly," "you are absolutely right" or "that's it," Socrates was boring. I have heard Bergson talk and he was another Socrates. The thoughts fell from his precise lips fully armed: if the interlocuter wanted to interrupt him, Bergson would say, *"Et alors, et alors . . ."* and continue reeling off his idea, an admirable, exact, velvet ribbon. But there would be no conversation.

My idea of conversation is a relaxation with sudden changes of subject and perspective, like that plaything of our grandfathers so aptly called the kaleidoscope, which with

56

each movement offered us new structures that were always symmetrical and always beautifully different. There are constant little shocks in conversations, such as a question, a witty word, a memory, an anecdote that is the very essence of gaiety, one of those "by the ways" indicating that we are going to speak of something altogether out of the way.

The strange thing is that after this brief change of horizon the conversation resumes, like a thin trickle of water flowing among the rushes. The result is that the order of conversation is an order of repetitions with excresences, digressions and avant-garde points; but this is never able to remove from the discourse its gravitational attraction.

And so it is necessary that our projects, our very thoughts be spun out, be *conversed* for a long time. I mean, of course, that we share them with a close friend, in the way that Goethe confided in Eckermann, and in the way that all men instinctively confide in women. For the woman is the agent of conversation by reason of her constantly desultory ramblings, her excessive affirmations, her repetitions, her serious, innocent intuitions. But whether it be a woman, a male companion (and sometimes a canary, a cat or a turtle, as happens among the lower classes) this echo of one's own words is useful. The advantage of constant conversation is that it never allows our thought to contract; conversation lets the thought unfurl and show its multiple faces. We discover that our ways of seeing are surrounded with questions or explanations; that they do not dissolve nor harden; that they never pass into the repressed zone of ourselves where the alert psychoanalyst discovers them in a state of refuse and decay.

That is why gossiping women talk constantly and why the masses converse as much as they can, until they are overcome by some great anger or by sleep. To chatter, to orate, to prattle is for many a hygiene of the soul. And when one travels for eight consecutive hours in a second-class train, this precipitation of confidences is bound to take place, not so much to overcome boredom, but so that each passenger may govern his own inner world by uncontrolled speech. Observe youngsters. They talk without waiting for the other to finish. And even with "grown-ups," conversation hardly has any real answers. That is not asked of it. But from the exchange of two thoughts, from the juxtaposition of two people, an atmosphere, a wisdom superior to both, a sort of slowly clearing sky is born.

13   *Elegance*

WHAT a pretty word! There is a joy in pronouncing it. It has an agile beginning and a resonance, which is like the lingering shadow of a passing bird.

This word, which we usually restrict to our dress, signifies much more. There is such a thing, for example, as moral elegance. All perfect morality is elegant; that is to say, one is morally elegant when, faced with a choice between several equally possible acts, one stops at the most discreet, the least showy, that which is becoming to oneself and only to oneself. It is possible to wear a suit or a dress with elegance; but then the elegance is in the movement of the muscles, the sway of the hips. Elegance is brought out in your choice of fabric, form, and color; elegant clothing becomes your coat of arms, by which others will recognize that this is indeed yourself. Elegance does not require luxuriousness or gold. A rag can be eminently elegant, as we see in Andalusia with the beggars.

A more secret, difficult, and improbable elegance is the elegance of thoughts which no one sees. Not to take offense at a malicious or evil word, not to brood over a failure, not to seek spiteful revenge, not to rejoice in another's misfortune, not to envy a good that comes another's way — how rare this is, how almost impossible for our nature!

It is noteworthy how the habits of religious become them. When a friar walks down the street, he attracts the eye of the artist; he makes people reflect on the loss to masculine dress since the gown ceased to be a spiritual symbol. The Sister of Charity with her beautiful white wings of yesteryear, her habit of blue so soft, yet sad, the blue of old France — who would dare to say that she did not teach that there was some connection between charity and elegance? It is an elegance which in these two cases is composed of a conformity between the folds of the material and the workings of the soul.

We understand, then, that elegance is not conferred by luxury but rather by poverty; the latter brings us closer to the state of nature where nothing is useless — not a flower, not a bee. And the most perfect elegance is seen in the woman who is satisfied with herself, who "wears well what she has" as does the lily of the field, that Galilean flower so sumptuous in the eyes of Christ.

A curious thing: have you not noticed, as I have, that in certain complicated cases of life, in order to know immediately what we should do, the thought of duty is not the first to come to mind? On the contrary, the idea of good taste does. Would it be elegant to act in this way? Of these two ways of acting, which one stands out before us as the most tasteful? I know some people, for example, who are more directly moved by the absence of elegance in certain sin of omission than by the idea of "offending God." But is there not more than one way of grasping this difficult Good, hidden in the cloud like all high places whose clearest reflection is seen in earthly beauty?

14 *Woman's Solitude*

I WOULD say that there are two kinds of solitude. There is the feeling of being alone which we experience — as young Proust did when his mother put him to bed at night without giving him a good-night kiss — when our ties with others grow weak. It would be better to call this solitude *isolation*.

But there is another, deeper solitude which consists in that, far from all other men and from our closest friends, we feel even farther from a heavenly society. We are strictly no longer on earth and neither, for that matter, are we in heaven. It is a sacred solitude. There enters into it what the Latins called *timor*; the pagans knew this solitude. Christianity alone exorcizes it or rather sublimates it because it turns it into an apprenticeship and a prayer.

If this distinction is admissible, we may ask ourselves whether women know these two forms of diminution better than men. And my answer is this:

The ties which women naturally form with nature and life, with their husbands, their children, other women, and with their household duties make them more closely united to the world than men are, more entrenched in the universe, more

temporalized; women have no vocation whatsoever to boredom. The desperate cries of despair have been uttered by men:
Job, Prometheus, Vigny, Nietzsche, Heidegger. These lamen-
tations are not considered to be womanly. Moans, groans
and revolt have their origin in man. And, on the other hand,
when the absence of normal relations with the outside world
vow a woman to what I have called *isolation,* immediately her
ability to adapt herself to the higher world, to deepen what
I called *solitude* comes into play. A woman has a strange faculty (strange at least to us men) of being at home both in per-
forming ordinary tasks and extraordinary ones. Mme. Acarie
had ecstasies when tossing an omelette. The omelette was perfect; so was the ecstasy. This would not have happened with
an ecstatic male chef! Joan of Arc leaped from ecstasy while
riding into battle. Through this perpendicular faculty which
joins the base with the summit, the woman can escape isolation, since she moors herself very quickly to the world, even if
through frivolity. She can also run away from isolation and
find her God again in solitude. The difference between Teresa
of Avila and John of the Cross is worth noting through the
use they made of solitude. Teresa was entirely at ease in it. Solitude was the atmosphere in which she spread her wings. Can
we say the same thing of John of the Cross? To be sure, he
longed to be alone — but in order to be purified by his black
fire.

But then, someone may say, how is it that in our present-
day world we meet so many women dismayed and in revolt?

This is due to the fact that, despite appearances, the modern world is not very well adapted to the happiness of wom-
en. It has only half loved her and liberated her. And nothing is
worse for an easily distressed being then to stop half
way. Surely, the modern world has emancipated women, it has
discovered her, it has honored, extolled and paid court to her;
it has proclaimed her basic equality with man: woman can
vote, they are officials, they are admitted into the organiza-

tions of men. We have women aviators, women military officers. But has this free woman emerged in a universe made for the blossoming of her femininity? Certainly not. The free woman makes her appearance in a world that is masculine to a high degree, a world created by the male — an analytical, administrative, intellectual, hard, sexual, sensual, warlike, lucid, powerful genius. It is a world endowed with institutions that have been masculine for centuries, steeped in a Greek and Judaic culture, but never anything but masculine. The captive woman of yesterday suffered from her imprisonment, but she breathed a feminine atmosphere. The modern woman is free but abandoned, plagued by the concurrence of man. Oh yes, men flatter women; they idealize them, they commiserate with them, they invent machines to help them; they give women diplomas, titles, and prizes. But do they love women for themselves? That is an entirely different matter.

This secret exchange of the present condition of women is less noticeable in the married woman and in the mother. But it explains the suffering of so many young women, of widows, of solitary women who seem to be happy because they *earn* their livelihood, but who are not happy because they do not *live* the life they earn, not having met the person who would have loved them, or the home in which they would have blossomed.

To this solitude, born of unfulfillment, there can be but one holy solution, preinscribed in the heart of woman who is made by nature to adore.

And while we thumb the album of *interior* women whose names history has preserved (I refer to women who lived an interior life without being nuns), this album which Victor Cousin, Sainte-Beuve and Brémond enriched with pastel drawings, we note these people of flesh and tenderness who were tried by solitude, even in the midst of the noises of the world, and who knew how to transform it into an evening sacrifice; for example, Mme. Desbordes-Valmore, Eugénie de

Guérin, Mme. Swetchine. Closer to our own times, there is Elizabeth Lesoeur or Marie-Noël. Even a George Sand, who is indeed the contrary of the isolated or solitary woman, only found herself at Nohant or at Gargilesse, where the solitude characteristic of the rural area which is, as it were, an image of the tranquility of God, pacified her.

15   *The Second Sex*

NO ONE can contest the talent of Simone de Beauvoir, and along with this talent her "courage," if courage consists in battling the most prevalent prejudices. She has recounted her life for us in three large books. She has handed over to us her own living commentary on her philosophy of love. This is a work in which she amasses, according to her compelling method, all that contributes to her thesis: biology, ethnology, the history of ideas and of morals, the testimony of literary men, and finally psychoanalysis; this to prove that, even in this day, the condition of woman is not the authentic one, because woman has been *subjected* and not *subject,* a slave, a myth invented by man and not a human person.

Two themes can summarize this plea of woman against man. The first is that, until now, woman has not been thought about by woman but by man, and therefore she has been thought of as "the other one." Moreover, man has idealized woman: he has not considered the real woman but rather the woman of his dreams, who serves as the occasion and receptacle for his myths. He has made woman a goddess, but only the better to make her a slave; he exalted her in his mind only to lower her in the ordinary routine of life. That is what happened in the past and it explains the present.

Mme. de Beauvoir shows us the *genesis* of woman from her childhood to her own discovery that she is a woman, to her experiences as a woman, maternity being the most common. Simone de Beauvoir follows woman through her menopause and on to old age. The conclusion of all this is that woman in the modern world is unhappy because society in its obedience to stupid customs has left her ignorant of the truth of her condition by not allowing her to know herself and to act accordingly.

The summary I have just made points out only the broad, abstract outline of the work; after all, under this form, the majority of those who reflected on the condition of woman in the world of yesterday could sign their name to the book. But two further remarks should be added.

This is the first time in history that this subject has been treated by a woman (and in a book destined for the general public) without shame. It is impossible to quote Mme. de Beauvoir without running the risk of making wheels grind. The author did not set out to be deliberately immodest (although she certainly weighed in accurate scales the advantage there was for the success of her book by constantly calling a spade a spade). Before her, books on women suffered from language inhibitions. Now that these interdicts have been jettisoned *by a woman,* we wonder whether or not they possessed a *raison d'être,* whether certain things, spelled out in public, are not in themselves unnatural. Yes, every reality whose essence it is to be mysterious loses its nature when it is laid bare, exposed, "exhibited" before our very eyes.

Mme. de Beauvoir's idea is that woman, insofar as she differs from man, is a product of manners and custom. Deep down in her being, the woman ought to be equal, comparable to man. And the insuperable boundaries which the organic responsibilities of the woman represent must be minimized as much as possible and made completely subject to the consent of woman. It goes without saying that all the institutions that have restricted the liberty of woman seem to Mme. de Beauvoir to be valueless shackles, especially that of marriage. Inversely, what morality calls vice can, to her way of thinking, be justified, provided the woman conducts herself toward it with freedom, with elegance of soul, and provided she takes the responsibility for these true-to-life situations upon herself. In brief, everything about woman is *custom* and not *nature*. Woman in her entirety is *condition* and not *essence*. All sexual morality is a *rule* of opinion and not *duty*.

Despite my deep desire to find an element of truth in this immense repertory and in Madame de Beauvoir's diatribe, I am embarrassed by her tone of insolence, in the etymological sense of the word. We respect her tragic history, which is read between the lines in the second volume under the guise of impersonal developments. Besides, the author criticizes less the condition of woman in herself than that of women in a certain bourgeois class whose narrowness I am as aware of as she is. I know the truth of her criticism regarding the ignorance in which girls are kept. We are as scandalized as she is to see the masculine species condemn prostitution and abortion and not reform the conduct that makes prostitution and abortion inevitable. There is a great deal of hypocrisy in the world, but the sexual sphere is that in which hypocrisy is perhaps the most worthy of hatred.

It is also our wish that love be free, that man and woman may choose each other, that they know what they are doing and why. I would also like to add that Mme. de Beauvoir's critics are not concerned with a Christian morality that is lived to perfection but with its pharisaic deformations. Perhaps cynicism is a defence of her heart against the hypocrisy of the flesh. With her we hope that the woman's hour is coming, that is, that the personality of woman may soon find the most favorable conditions for blossoming. I will even go so far as to admit that Mme. de Beauvoir has a clear insight into the fact that "sex" was, for man as well as for woman, only a temporal situation, and therefore a temporary one; that we were not sexed in the deepest strata of our soul. Sex is an original condition of our historical being for which we must also assume responsibility. *Does not the Christ of St. Luke say that in the hereafter there will no longer be men or women and that we will be like angels, being sons of the resurrection?* Mme. de Beauvoir makes me feel all this independence of our eternal being with respect to the conditions of its passing. She makes me feel them with strong proofs, with a sort of masculine candor which is not foreign to so independent a genius. For she is a serious woman more than an erudite one.

But where I cannot follow her (and where she herself has difficulty in doing so) is in the numerous passages which introduce a sacred horror for what in woman's condition is most constant, most noble: *maternity*. Here, Mme. de Beauvoir (whom I think is not a mother and has no desire to be one) sees only subjection to desires, to difficult necessities. She has that distrust regarding motherhood which Gabriel Marcel already pointed out regarding Jean-Paul Sartre on the matter of fatherhood.

The reason is that *fatherhood* and *motherhood* (that is to say the two forms of incarnate love on earth) cannot be justified in an atheistic perspective. Mme. de Beauvoir's desire is to understand everything without God and to justify everything without God: to desire pure freedom without God. Now, if true motherhood consists in consent, there is in maternity an absence of choice in regard to many things. . . . We can, to be sure, diminish this absence; but we will never entirely suppress it.

It seems to me that the biological infirmities of woman's condition are of little weight compared to the responsibility of carrying the body of the future man, of presenting him to the world, of nourishing him with her substance, preserving him, offering him, molding his first consciousness. The mother is his first model of humanity and of pure love. The degradations of her role dissipate before this royal honor which even the pagans held in high esteem.

He who says "mother" says *creation* or rather *co-operation* in the work of creation; he who says "mother" says *consent* to the unknown action of the Creator of every being, who alone chooses the moment and the ways. He who thinks that the duty of man is to assert his complete freedom cannot understand what I have just said. It is to be feared that such a person may destroy not only the femininity of woman but even the humanity of man and woman. According to the cruel and profound words of one of Sartre's characters: "I am free *for nothing*."

Surely, the long periods of history in which the person of woman has been obliterated, subjected and sacrificed without reserve to her function of child-bearing appear somber and deserving of criticism on more than one point.

But in the supposition that the principles of Mme. de Beauvoir were to receive social and political application, what monster would we be preparing for ourselves in this completely lucid and choosing woman, whose love in an inhabited flesh would be exclusively intelligence?

Surely, Mme. de Beauvoir had the courage to bring out into full daylight the problem of intelligence as it is incarnated in the body of woman. So many modern prophets are laboring to cultivate woman's intelligence without ever suspecting its disadvantages! At least this time the problem is posed: To what condition can intelligence be incarnate? To accept the weight of flesh and life? For our author, intelligence protests against femininity, against motherhood.

Yes, I am not unaware of this problem. It is the whole purpose of this book: how many transformations have yet to be introduced if femininity is to become fully free, likewise if motherhood is to take place without humiliation and constraint, if man is to stand by woman fully instead of merely using her! But the root of the problem is elsewhere.

I asked myself the source of that sacred horror of motherhood on the part of the intellectual woman — such at least as motherhood has been practiced for forty centuries, if not from the beginning. The reason lies in the fact that fatherhood and motherhood can be lived profoundly, but cannot fully justify themselves in an atheistic context. If we deny the reality of him from whom all paternity in heaven and on earth receives its law and honor by way of delegation, it becomes very difficult to conceive why one must accept being a father or a mother (or a child), since in this matter we have no choice. We must accept the day of birth, its manner, the sex of the child, his personality. And the child likewise accepts this father, his mother, these brothers and sisters whom he has not freely chosen. Against these constraints, the woman-made-free revolts. In this matter she would like *pure* freedom. She would like to be God and create. But instead, woman's freedom lies in her ability to procreate, a word that so well bespeaks the function in which she acts as the creator who, so to speak, helps the Creator of all natures. I agree that without this belief, for a mind that follows its thoughts to their logical conclusion, woman is absurd and her being a mother is incomprehensible.

16 *The Assassin and the Saint*

PERHAPS you remember hearing of a young Italian girl and of her strange experience. Only twelve years old, she resisted an attacker, but he overpowered her. As she struggled under his hold, she told him that she did not want to commit sin, that she preferred death.

Civil justice was implacable; the assassin was sentenced to thirty years in prison. God's justice was merciful, unexpected. The murderer repented, and after having been released from prison, lead a religious life. Meanwhile, the village pastor had called Rome's attention to this new Agnes; a process of canonization was begun, and later Maria Goretti was inscribed in the catalog of the saints. Her executioner attended the ceremony of her triumph. We may divine what his feelings were. If the text "for those who love God all things work together unto good" (Rom. 8,28) took on meaning, it was for this man.

The other day I happened to be in the company of a few friends who were discussing this very story. I sensed embarrassment. One girl said: "That's what you would call acquiring sanctity the easy way." She added, with a sort of timid regret that made us smile "It seems to me that I would have acted exactly as Maria did, and that now I would be a saint. . . . Instead, I will have to work at it day by day, becoming mediocre in the daily grind, and finally I will die uncertain, unknown . . . ." We reassured her as best we could.

It is true that in the realm of genius there are favored people; eleventh-hour laborers, they arrive when the others have toiled, apparently in vain. They arrive, I say, with the smile of one who knows beforehand that he has won. They throw their net exactly the same way as the others; they make a catch; they carry off everything. There are some who redeem themselves bit by bit in the course of a long, monotonous life. Others pay in gold all at once.

This would be unjust if poor, ordinary men were defrauded to the benefit of these heroes. I believe, on the contrary, that they gain. The moral of Maria Goretti's death is that an act of love, when well made, carries off the infinite. In this singular case, the act bore fruit without ripening. This shows us, in a special way, the value of every act inspired by pure duty. I would not go so far as to say that this act placed the young girl outside of humanity but, quite the contrary, that it lifts all humanity up to her, that it enables us to see in her what is hidden in the ordinary routine of the world.

The extraordinary is a sample taken from the ordinary which routine veils from us; the sublime is the profound of every day. Yes, what Maria Goretti accomplished for all to see is what many do in this world in obscurity. But *in her,* this obscurity becomes illumined, the multitude of humble people are glorified in her. At each moment of time, God sees innumerable acts as pure as that of Maria's, and these acts exist forever in what Joubert called God's memory. . . . It was with thoughts of this nature that I tried to reassure the somewhat jealous girl who had asked the first question.

But another young girl rose and made a pertinent remark. She remarked that, if Maria Goretti had been completely ignorant of sex (as my young friend said she was at twelve due to the policy of her parents), she would never have been able to have had complete control over her mind to make the act of refusal which merited the glory of sainthood. Piety therefore has a certain knowledge of evil as its prerequisite, and this knowledge is often not given out of a sense of false prudence. I believe that everyone unanimously agreed in condemning the old method (more true of the bourgeois than of lower-class people), which deprived youth of the possibility of knowing themselves, when out of reticence it hid from them the mystery of their body.

Then a young man, who attempted to be subtle, asked the inevitable question: "If this madman had not tempted and then killed this Italian girl, heaven would be minus two saints. So . . . "

I leave it to you to fill in the conclusion which this terrible philosopher reached with the intransigence of youth. My answer was that we must beware of injecting ourselves into God's way of acting. To draw good from evil, the best from the worst, pertains to God alone. As for ourselves and *the future,* our role must to avoid what is evil and not imitate that assassin in order to become, thirty years later, a good man and the author of a saint. As for *the past,* we should help actual grace to utilize even our sins in order to give depth to our soul. As for *the present,* we must offer its greatness by our good intentions. The act of assassination on this frail and pure victim was that of Cain, that of every sinner. Who has not perpetrated it? And who has not later on been aware that the Repairer had drawn a very improbable good out of it?

The story also teaches that we must never be too hasty in judging. Violence, incomprehensible injustice, downfalls, scandals — everything is an enigma, an ambiguous source for better or for worse before the final day of discernment.

And lastly this story suggests the grandeur of intransigence. In the eyes of men and of the "wise" and "prudent" of this world, this young girl ought to have yielded, ought to have acquiesced to this "true-to-life situation" of violence. She could have compromised. The threat of death would excuse her weakness. And nothing would have changed in the world: no crime, no assassin, only a very banal incident such as occurs every harvest-time. Yes, this is all very true; but had this line of reasoning been used the conscious world would be minus one light and, consequent upon such a lame excuse, there would have been a little less strength and grace for good. But as it now stands, the story of Maria Goretti will bring forth fruit in thousands of consciences. It will ever be the model to follow. And from the sole telling of it, it is a secret source of help.

The world is saved when a few have the courage to lay down absolute limits, inviolate to any compromise. Fortunately, this equivocal world is still blessed with some of these intransigent souls who prefer, if need be, to die rather than yield a principle of justice or truth.

There is an analogy between the indomitable character of Maria and the office of the Roman Pontiffs, namely to erect impassable boundaries before recurring human errors, to remind us of certain unchangeable principles. And that is evidently why we always note, and this from the earliest days of the Church, the indescribable tenderness of the Popes for these pampered daughters, for these virgins of the Italian race who did nothing more than keep themselves pure . . . for Agnes, Cecilia, Lucy, and Anastasia, who are commemorated every day in the Roman Mass.

17 *The Crisis of Conjugual Love*

WHEN two people live a communal life which permits of no privacy, no solitude whatsoever, in which no counterfeiting is possible, there comes a moment when they can no longer not know each other. An inversion occurs. And acumen, instead of discovering the heretofore unknown virtues of each other, brings to light the faults, the manias, the imperfections, in a word all that was necessarily hidden in the first phase of love and which now seems all the more evident. These are not so much large faults or vices as rather trifling mediocrities, indistinguishable insincerities — in short, the inevitable dust of every virtue and of every existence.

This is also the time when the wife is less beautiful, due to habit (beauty is composed partly of surprise), due to her discomforts and her confinements, and also because she feels that she is loved less dearly (beauty is composed in part of the idea that we are loved). Renewal is no longer possible. The marriage vows and society have bound you together forever. Forever ... always ... how harsh these words are for the person who still has an entire lifetime before him! Can we not make another choice and, as they say, "begin life all over again?" Is it a duty to renounce one's happiness forever? The feeling of the irreparable leads to self-accusations which are always more difficult to bear than accusations against others. "You say that I am not the one you thought I was," Robert says to Evelyne in Gide's *Ecole des Femmes,* "but neither are you what I thought you were." Then Evelyne says: "All there is left for me is to put myself at the disposal of someone for whom I have no more love, no more esteem . . . at the disposal of the nonentity whose wife I am. That is my lot, my reason for existence, my goal, and I have no other horizon on earth."

This crisis differs in man and in woman.

When the man becomes aware of his first deceptions, he feels his instinct awaken within him, for it is more passionate and less fixed on one person then the woman's. Even from the physical point of view the wife is more faithful than the husband; impregnated by a man, she remains his. It is through sentiment that she turns to adultery. She does this more because of a great boredom than because of sensuality. It also happens that a sort of second sexuality is awakened belatedly in the woman. Doctors and psychiatrists of our era are now becoming aware of what formerly was only hinted at by novelists or painful confidences, a drama imbedded in a nature incarnated in flesh.

It sometimes happens that the woman's senses are not awakened until several years after her marriage, perhaps even after she has fulfilled her maternal role. If at this time she meets a person who arouses these new feelings, a wound can develop in her soul, as Balzac showed in his *Lys dans la Vallée,* where the insolent kiss of a very young man troubles the pure Henrietta in the deep recesses of her soul. Yes, the more inoffensive the man seems, the more dangerous he is; for the first unconscious unfaithful movements have the appearance of platonic love. Woman is so quickly caught in the trap of pity. Man sometimes is, too, as we can see in Gide's *Symphonie*

Pastoral. It is in this latter book that we observe that sacred law which bends the home in on itself, which forces it to seal itself on its secrets.

In middle years, the husband is in the prime of life; he grows young again in his work, whereas the hard labor of the woman makes her grow old before her time. This premature aging effect is less apparent in the bourgeois world of our cities because of make-up, the artifices of style and the manner of living. But we see it in the country. The woman on a farm takes on the trappings of old age very quickly. In olden times, as she approached thirty, the French country-woman went to the wardrobe and took out the coif that she was to wear until death; it signified that from then on she gave up trying to look young, for she was nothing more than the senior servant of the master. Joubert at that time said, regarding his wife: "I took stock of both her merits and charms, but she preserved only her merits." It is true that man, too, loses some of his early comeliness. His work brings on wrinkles and stiffness. Specialization develops some of his faculties to the detriment of the others. Michelet contrasts the modern with the ancient man who preserved a happy equilibrium: "Penelope recognized Ulysses by his beauty, which neither his labors nor his travels had impaired."

18 *Start All Over?*

SOME married people go through crises that shatter love forever. The thought occurs to them of starting life all over with someone else, and the thought is all the more tempting when life has been a disappointment and there is still time to begin all over again. We are living in an age when almost all loves go through an evitable test because love is subject to the law of endurance.

It is so tempting to resolve it by transforming love into an association, union into a juxtaposition, the household into a grouping of mediocre interests, a married couple into the enlightened friendship of two former lovers united solely from habit. It is the hour when egoisms and attachments divide. The man goes to business, the woman to her tasks; the man to his labor, to his factory; the middle-class woman to her fashions and recipes; the man to his club, the woman to her bridge. Love languishes more easily as it is replaced by a state where appearances are kept up. Saint-Beuve expressed this stiffening of our beings so well when he said of himself: "We harden on certain points, we rot on others; we do not mature."

Many maturities are false and are only shams. How many

79

man are considered mature, who themselves think they are, but in reality are only adolescents in the guise of precocious old men? This prolongation of the ardor and the intractableness of adolescence during second childhood may have useful results in the field of arts, politics, and pleasure; but the fact that a fermentation might perhaps be profitable does not change its nature.

To mature is to let time accomplish its work of peace in us. It consists in being young at heart at that very time when the body is growing weak. From the point of view of love, maturity ought to be less a transformation than a fulfillment. It is sometimes said that the first heat of love is changed into friendship; if that is the case, the change would be great and for the worse. It would be a retrogression. The difficult task consists in seeing to it that lovers become also friends, without ceasing to be lovers!

How many marriages are nothing more than companionships in which two people who were formerly in love (or thought they were) outlive this first state? The profound difference between passion and sentiment here becomes evident. Love begins with a phase of emotion; only after a long period of time can it change into sentiment. This sentiment is a habit of the soul. But we must remember that there are two habits; one is pure automatism, mechanical and unconscious; the other is a kind of ever more perfect self-awareness, an awakening of hidden components. This aptitude is not far removed from sentiment. Sentiment dwells in us without our always being conscious of it. But at the least provocation it makes itself known under the guise of a tender and at the same time a very sweet emotion. Instead of sweeping us off our feet, as does passion or budding love, sentiment brings us back to ourselves.

In this second phase, love turned sentiment has less need of external expression. It is embedded less in the body than at that juncture where the soul and body are seamed together.

START ALL OVER?

In the beginning, both parties clung to the angelic side of each other. The other partner was regarded as perfect. Love's only salvation is to become a love of the incarnate and total being of the other partner, with all his deficiencies and his mediocrities. No one is asked to love the other's faults, but rather to love the other partner so much that his faults are considered as an almost negligible consequence of his incarnation.

Early in marriage, joys, travel, pleasures, gifts and celebrations — the magic of life — were necessary to weave the cloth of love. Later on, sickness, failures, bereavement and bitterness become the cementing forces of union.

Sorrow is more conducive to the awareness of living and of union than is pleasure. We should also note that this renaissance, or rather this metamorphosis, of love is made easier by the joint idea of success or glory. In his *Discourses,* Pascal says that a life is beautiful when it begins with love and finishes with ambition, all love growing in a great and shared ambition. The story of Heloïse and Abélard portrayed an Heloïse more jealous for the glory of Abélard than Abélard himself was. Often this is the innate reflex of woman. We sometimes see her, at this period of life, making a fine puppet out of her husband whom she pushes forward in the world, whose career she assures. For at this age man is the epitome of laziness, but the wife is ambitious for him. He would be satisfied to remain a colonel, but she wants him to be a general. On the other hand, it is at this moment that the man discovers the wifely merits which make their appearance beneath the faded charms, and he begins to praise the *strong woman*.

Then it is that new bonds, a new and reciprocal esteem is woven. Love blossoms again. Is there any reason to beg forgiveness if a new bond is formed?

19 *Love Wears Thin*

IN TRYING to console a woman who had renounced marriage, Fénelon said to her: "Let us not take into account the great number of marriages where scandalous dissensions abound. Rather let us concentrate on the best ones: to all external appearances there is nothing unfortunate about them; but how much do the husband and wife put up with in order to avoid open clashes!

"Let us even presume that both partners are equally reasonable people — a very rare and unhoped for blessing; yet both of them have their prejudices, their habits, their attachments . . . . They see each other at such close range, so often, with so many faults on the part of each other, in the most natural and the most unexpected occasions where advanced preparation is impossible. Their love begins to wear thin; imperfection repulses, their humanness is more and more brought home to them; they must at all times have control over themselves and not let it be seen."

Fénelon highlights an essential problem of marriage; but he takes unfair advantage of a true situation: he does not try to find the true solution.

To begin with, marriage is not the only vocation in life where the first fervor wears off. He uses Oxyrhynchus as an example. Oxyrhynchus was a city of Egypt that had been turned into a monastery. As we follow him there, do we not still hear its complaints? Monastic life has its gloominess, its repugnances and tribulations of soul. One's companions weigh heavily. Imperfection in oneself, in one's neighbor, and in one's superiors is very disheartening. But why draw up a longer list? Fénelon knew these things better than anyone — he who, although a bishop, suffered so much from the boredom of the world and the tedium of life. Such is the state of the child of Adam, regardless of his condition. To be sure, a mediocre marriage can rekindle this boredom, and deception can make us conscious of it; but we are making quick work of the matter when we see marriage and the perpetual proximity of the other spouse as its sole cause.

Moreover, a distinction must be made between the sanctity *of* the state and sanctity *in* the state. No Christian denies that the religious state is a more perfect life than the married state. But to be higher and more meritorious must it be devoid of inconveniences and graced with advantages? Fénelon's thesis consists of telling nuns that, humanly speaking, they have chosen the better part in having renounced the encumbrances of this world. Is his argument so religious after all? A book on the spirituality of the layman — and I am here trying to lay down its principles — must of necessity comprise a basic chapter entitled: *Making use of inconveniences.*

It nevertheless remains that marriage, being by nature and law indissoluble save by the death of one of the spouses, locks a person into a society that can become very difficult if love is absent. It is a law of the heart that when love recedes, it is not replaced by a state of indifference; without compassion, it would quickly end in hatred. One must live with the spouse who is no longer loved; hear him sneeze, chew his food. . . . My only comment about these dramas that are so common in the world is that they should serve as a warning to young people tempted to enter into marriage without an esteem that is much stronger than a brief passion, a marriage in which there is no community of thoughts, no similar traditions, no deeply shared faith. Yes, love can wear thin, but these latter bonds abide; in fact, are they so very different from love? Is it not true that love is the blurred intuition of these multiple correspondences between two people, which will become more and more apparent with the falling of the leaves and the wear and tear of time?

But let us return to the most ordinary case: that of a married couple who have lived together a decade (the peak of the tenth year is important in marriage) and who, without being estranged or parted, no longer retain the first fervor of their wedding day or at least no longer feel that once mutual admiration.

Common sense and experience in the art of loving will tell them that they must keep love alive, just as one keeps friendship alive. Furthermore, they will do this by doing little things for each other, by helping each other, by tender ingenuity in small matters, by forgetting, by reviving memories. There is a liturgy of love. And liturgy indeed teaches that it is a question of repeating the same rhythms, of beginning again what is unique and has no possible rebeginning, just as a priest each day offers a sacrifice that took place only once.

Then too, we must go one step further and contemplate human nature. What is a virtue, and what is a defect? Some people, it is said, have the defects of their virtues. But defect and virtue are often two aspects of the same kind of person. I observed this in World War I. When Joffre stopped being lucky, his calm was called indolence; when Foch had not yet won, his aggressive will was called impulsiveness. And Lyautey's pluck was sometimes daring, sometimes foolhardiness. You must pardon my examples taken from the realm of war. They are the image of what we see every day. The fault of a spouse is a virtue which I have ceased to love. The virtue of a spouse is his defect when I love him. We see this rather clearly in education where to love, not to love, or to love a child less, changes his nature.

And finally, let us talk of a great mystery. The differences of temperament that we note in conjugal life are the school of a truer love. Fénelon, who was disillusioned, brings this out in his haughty, calm way. He writes: "Complacency diminishes, the heart dries up, both spouses become a cross for each other; we love our cross, but it is nonetheless a cross which we must carry." I would prefer to say: It is not right to close our eyes to the opportunities for suffering that present themselves to us, but instead to foresee them and to utilize them. It is in these circumstances that we learn to know ourselves well: we see ourselves naked, without any mask whatsoever. When there is a marital conflict, there is no secret place where we can go to cry and reform our characteristics. We are projected one before the other without a shadow in which to hide. There is no monastic cell. The experience teaches us to love each other as we really are, to accept each other, to love each other not only despite our defects, but even because of them. Our defects are not only marks of failures of the will but also a sounding of the depths of the person, which love enables us to love in the other. Cardinal Saliège said to the people of Toulouse: "Above all, keep your defects, for through them you are loved." There is some truth in this sally of a happy bishop.

In marriage we again find that three quarter time according to which all the loves of this earth, and even divine love on earth, develop.

It begins with surprise, contentment, and easy habits. Time passes. Nature reasserts itself. And, as Fénelon said, love wears thin. Clashes, deceptions, even doubts arise . . . .But after the clouds, there is growth in that virtue which is "patient, is kind . . . . is not self-seeking" — the virtue St. Paul calls charity

(1 Cor. 13, 4,6). This rhythm, composed of an initial knowledge, of suffering due to that knowledge, and finally of a profound and peaceful knowledge, belongs to all that is lasting, of all that is seed for eternity. There exist, I know, even happier unions where this rhythm is scarcely visible; where souls live in perfect harmony, where they resemble each other; where nothing causes astonishment or comes as a surprise; where daily pardon has no place because there is no offense. This state generally occurs in the early days of the marriage, and also for a great many toward the end of their marriage. In marriage, Victor Hugo said, to grow old is to become identified.

20 *Common Consent*

THE opening sentence of the epistle read at a marriage ceremony reminds wives that they "should be submissive to their husbands as though to the Lord" (Eph. 5,22).

But no one is unaware of the fact that if the man reigns in the home, the woman rules, because she knows that art of penitents and mystics, which is to have someone tell her or advise her to do what pleases her. The woman has a hundred and one ways of circumventing the commands she does not want to hear. It is so easy to obey the letter of the law in such a way as to show how absurd the order was. For example, the husband tells his wife that a cabinet should be moved and she objects to it. So she moves it in such a way that it breaks, and everyone says: "The cabinet was better where it was." And so on. We all know families where the husband exercises only nominal authority.

And why complain, if he is happy with his lot? We are wrong in saying that it is man's destiny to command. In the army, how many officers are there whose main duty is to receive orders, to spring to attention, or, as we say, to protect themselves from responsibilty? How few of them seek to use initiative, which is successful disobedience! For there to be so many submissive men and so many governing women, women must also have the gift of governing. The proof of this is the many women of good works, abbesses and superiors who are more imperious than men. And having served under a nurse who was a major, I am convinced that male administration is better. Women are harder on their subordinates!

I have spent too much energy proving what everyone already knows: that women can still rule under the appearance of subordination. M. de Montmoran said in speaking of Teresa of Avila that she set out to find "the confessor who approved of her" — a remark I heard Bergson confirm following his study of the mystics. But the truth lies in a third point. The husband should not be the authoritarian head nor the wife an insinuating governess. One should not issue sharp orders nor should the other evade them. What commands both of them and what they both serve, although in a different way, is the common good which the husband should clearly decree and which the wife must evoke in language of the heart. They should determine first of all what this common good is, using common consent.

But you will ask, how is this common consent reached? In small communities, common consent is reached by oral exchanges, by conversations between those in authority, in which the head gives his opinion, then listens to the different opinions of the others, takes up his own again and adapts it until a common opinion results. Now in a household, there are countless opportunities to communicate, to exchange points of view. We may even say that married life is a conversation that is scarcely interrupted by the night stars and that begins all over again with the dawn. To harmonize points of views between two people whose goals, sentiments or habits are so closely knitted together should not be impossible, especially if we presuppose that friendship, wisdom and love bind the couple together. Under these conditions, marital authority neither needs to manifest itself nor does feminine deviousness have to prevail. To be sure, the man sees things better from the point of view of reason and law. But the woman is better at divining what will succeed and what will fail. She is less hampered by rules. From this blending there results a happy medium, which has the greatest chance of being right.

21   *Incompletion*

MAN and woman are incomplete, but not in the same way. In creating the human being, God did not make an androgynous creature who would be self-sufficient, as in hermaphroditic flowers. He stopped with this deficient form, incomplete in all its parts, which we call sex. But this halving is not limited solely to the body, as is generally believed; it includes every faculty, every nuance, every detail.

Man is by nature incomplete. In man more than in woman, nature seems to have grown weary of completing its work; it left man insatiable, greedy, tormented, striving to undertake, to build, and to improve things. He is constantly busy making or remaking. And his actions are often unsatisfied exercises. He takes refuge in war as in a horrible solution. Despite what is said, down deep there is something in the male make-up that delights in war, something there which answers the male desire to destroy, to project, to use trickery, to reckon, to displace himself every day; for even in siege, war is movement. Cries of discontent, from Oedipus to Job, have been uttered by man and his uneasy works, such as those of Pascal, Kierkegaard or of Blondel. The idea of sin came to man first.

INCOMPLETION

Eve and Magdalene saw only good in the fruit. Only afterward did they cry. Up until now the field of creative art has been practically closed to women. (How few women have invented new forms, whereas they invent the child with each birth?) And this is so, undoubtedly, because a woman is more easily satisfied than man and because invention presupposes a basic restlessness.

What woman lacks is the ability to awaken herself: she needs an encounter in order to be freed, and this generosity that has no definite object weighs on her and suffocates her. She wants to give and she cannot. The door through which she would like to be able to give must be broken down by man, that beggar; she cannot open it by herself. She can inspire, but she must first be incited. There is something tragic, from the biological order all the way to the mystical, in this condition of the woman who has almost but not quite everything in her that could make her self-sufficient. She stops just short of parthenogenesis, deprived of that incitement which man alone possesses, the secret hidden within himself, in his flesh, in his soul.

Faced with this antithesis, some might be inclined to think that progress could reform this and bring it about that man will calm himself by himself and that woman will incite herself by herself. But as soon as man rests, he falls into dull torpor. And a woman who incites herself and excites herself becomes passionate, agitated, fantastic and unbalanced, unbearable to others and herself. The completion of these incompleted beings requires nothing more than their love. But total love presupposes that the incompleteness of the one, like a well-made key, will have the exact form of the incompleteness of the other. And this demands, along with an initial grace, fifty years of work and of welcome.

For it is a profound and invincible error to think, as lovers do, that marriage is the solution to love. Marriage poses a problem: a whole life is scarcely long enough to resolve it. Marriage is not so much the effect of the often hasty love of the betrothed, who understand each other well, but knew each other poorly — who perhaps never get to know each other as husband and wife. Marriage is a seed. Marriage is the cause of a love that continues to develop throughout the lifetime of the couple, in a punctuated way, interspersed with crises, slow, vulnerable, admirable.

It happens that I am reading a study by Raymond Escholier on the marriage of Victor Hugo. What precious lessons can be gleaned from this delightful and tragic story! How these two young people who believed they were made for each other complemented each other so poorly! Recalling the day of their marriage, Lamartine was to write to Madame Hugo:

"The day this bridegroom, like a drunken harvester,
  Brings you to this cottage, hand in hand . . . ."

Hugo's mistake lay in considering the day of his marriage as one of completion, whereas it was only a beginning.

22   *A Communion of Hearths*

PATRIARCHAL economy obliged newlyweds to live under the common roof. The father of the family, the *pater-familias* of the old Roman law, was the absolute master of this community. He ruled over his sons and their wives. All new couples were under his jurisdiction. Such a regimen was favorable to farming, which needs varied and collective hands. We still see this in some European farming areas, where the son who marries brings his young bride to the common hearth where she must live with her mother-in-law and sisters-in-law, who accept her and bear with her without too much complaint. For there is work to be done — work that is ever pressing, always shared, work that is done in common under the relentless sun.

Christ's command that a man leave his father and mother was indeed a strange one. It implied that the human person was lawfully released from belonging to the group and that, by reason of their marriage, husband and wife might set up a new hearth.

That is what we see nowadays. Sometimes necessity still forces newlyweds to seek asylum in their parent's home. In our day, such cohabitation is hardly to be counseled because of the unnecessary wear and tear on the heart. Whose fault is it? It is difficult to say: experience proves that women who are not of the same family find it difficult not to chafe each other.

In the West, homes are tending to become more and more independent, stars that twinkle all by themselves and of which one could say:

> Every woman is very far
> From the sisters whom you think her neighbor to.
> Her caressing and delicate brightness . . .

burns for her alone. Love that jealously concentrates on itself loses its power by closing in upon itself. It also becomes more impoverished because when in need it can no longer obtain help easily.

Naturally there is a temptation to group families together along lines that are more voluntary and supple than the old patriarchal way.

A village of which I am very much a part comes to mind. It is to be found in the center of France, almost half-way between the pole and the equator, between the ocean and the Alps. The only invaders ever to reach it were the English, and that was during the Hundred Years' War. Life goes on almost as it did in the Neolithic age when man lived there on a rocky ridge bordering a lazy river. The church is two and a half miles from here, the railroad station ten miles. This village has no grocery, no school, nothing which generally serves to embody community life. It is purely and simply a grouping of seven hearths.

Neighborliness is a thing of the past in our cities. In the metropolis we can everlastingly ignore the neighbor who lives on the same floor as we do, even if he is more Christian than we are; we meet him with his missal under his arm without even knowing his name. But in the country, especially in a group of isolated homes without communal ties, social contacts between neighbor and neighbor such as mutual aid, solidarity, friendship, *agape* in all its forms, become almost necessary for life. These are unstable contacts — just as is everything that is based on sentiment — affinities that may reverse themselves. As a result, instead of a community of friendship and mutual aid we may find feelings of mistrust, of silence and indifference which are all the more painful to bear the closer the people live together. Poor human hearts!

I have often thought that the task of our century was to recapture community foundations by lifting them up to the spiritual plane. These groupings of homes which reasons of defense or mutual help imposed on man as soon as he made his appearance on earth symbolize spiritual communions, unfettered by space and juxtaposition. Christian groups that unite mankind through mutual aid and the *agape* in this arid modern world are similar to those huddles of the first human families.

And these groups of families dispersed in space form a spiritual community, which used to be called a religious society, a sodality, a congregation; the terminology means little. The essence of religious association consists in being a *communion* of persons living the same kind of material and spiritual life with one and same purpose of cooperating in the coming of God.

Heretofore we have known only formal religious associations made up of individuals. To avoid individualism, it was necessary to impose severe rules of obedience and generally (the individuals being by definition without families) a common material existence. But we can conceive of new associations that are no longer composed of individuals but of homes, of small families that do not live a common material life but who nevertheless have a similar existence and convergent preoccupations. We can presuppose families of lawyers, industrialists, professors, farmers, and politicians who would propose to each other the same ideal and who would group themselves together in one communion of spirit.

This seems to be very difficult to organize. To begin with, people who remain in the world are asked to practice the virtues of those who barricade themselves, who put themselves outside the reach of the world and its temptations. It is a fact that in the crude societies of yesteryear where, for example, an isolated girl risked her honor, where no one was sure that his house would not be violated during the night, it was wise to seek shelter behind a stone wall and visible discipline. Moreover, before the day of the postal service, the telephone and the newspaper, before radio and television, before the rocket, men *could not live the same life without being under the same roof.* On the other hand, we are more autonomous than our father: we can have the spirit of discipline and even of intelligent obedience without receiving formal orders from a superior. In the last analysis, what is a command? Pascal said: "If God were to give us direct orders, oh! how glady we would obey him. Necessity and everyday happenings are God's infallible orders." To these must be added what the Seventeenth Century understood so poorly: the duties of one's state in life, the rules of conjugal life, the formation of children and civic duties — are not these obligations that are even more demanding than the commandments and everyday happenings themselves, because they demand constant thought, responsibility, initiative, and solitude on our part?

Groups of homes are one of those novelties of the Spirit which point to a kind of springtime in our world. New and still unnamed flowers are appearing. They remind the connoisseur of some very old species, and yet they are unknown. We watch them appear with tender anxiety and with an almost unquestioning hope.

23   *An Evening at Nazareth*

IN THE house where I spent my vacation one summer there was a picture on the wall by an unknown artist. It bore the inscription: *Evening at Nazareth.*

The painter had represented Mary and Joseph seated beside each other in a small garden enclosed by a rather low wall which formed a terrace. It was evening, that uncertain hour. In that high place where Renan wanted a temple erected to the idea of Man, the violet brow of Carmel faces the western sea. To the east is Thabor and its solitary dome, as is the Puy-de-Dôme in the background of our open country in the center of France. Mary and Joseph are looking absent-mindedly at the arid mountains, that is, toward Jerusalem which one could reach *per montana* after a three days' walk. Joseph and Mary are seated; they are calm, relaxed, and tired, like workers at the end of the day. They are watching the Child with a kind of uneasiness. He is resting his elbow on the terrace, looking toward the south in deep contemplation. The Child has already made his first pilgrimage to Jerusalem: there he was lost and found. Since then, he looks like one who is going up to Jerusalem, the city that kills prophets. There was a peacefulness about this picture but also something indefinably agonizing and serious, as in a familiy where the son or the daughter of the house has already let it be known that they are going to sever their connections with it. The details of the departure are not known. We respect their silence. But this peace savors of something that will soon come to an end: it is enjoyed solely as a halt by the wayside.

In this picture I divine the criss-crossing of three kinds of authority. Reflection on the Holy Family has long given rise to thoughts on authority. Leo XIII loved this subject of meditation.

According to the absolute eternal order, the Child is king here. All three sense it and know it. But rule of *divine humiliation* will that the Child be subject.

According to the social and legal order, Joseph is the head of the family. He is the one who decides when to travel and when to return, the Abraham who leads and whom all see.

According to the order of the inner life, of interior truth and of privilege, the Virgin rules since she is the only one from whom the Child proceeded.

Each of them can look upon themselves as inferior or superior to the other depending on the point of view. In this particular community there is fulfilled to the highest degree the maximum of charity in which each one honors the other as greater than himself. And yet, in the realm of depths, it is the Child who governs all in secret and who is the foundation of the authority of the others.

Superior to the others, but subject to all, such is the definition of the head in all regions of life. He commands, he has the right to be obeyed; but he in turn is commanded and he obeys. Whom does he obey? God, you will answer. Yes, that is true; but between God and him there is as it were a relay: the general interest, the common good, the community of which he is a member and which has confided to him its own inevitable self-consciousness. The mind of the ruler is the place where this community decides what is fitting for it. And the role of the ruler is to have his eyes anxiously riveted on what this common good demands every instant.

In the same way in the evenings at Nazareth, the Virgin had her eyes fixed on the Child-King, the embodiment of the people of God and also of a new people, the culmination of the entire Church, of the Church growing under its germinal form. The Virgin asked herself what he who always obeyed her demanded of her.

And the only day he did not obey, during the stay at Jerusalem, she understood, in surprise that it was because he belonged to a supreme community. Then, in her mind, the idea of the common Good took on a wider meaning.

This often happens in the life of those in authority. They discern good according to their own standards. For example, a father and mother work hard to insure the health of their child. But lo! the child falls sick; he dies. What disobedience! They must rise to a higher plane and understand that the only final good of a community is that which links it without any intermediary to the divine Will: and hence that parodoxical, unconditional, apparently absurd but most reasonable obedience is possible, the obedience of Abraham in the act of immolating his son Isaac.

This is tantamount to saying that the head of the family is not a privileged person set apart from those who obey him, receiving honors, a man who is a law unto himself, who reduces others to the inferior condition of slaves, subjects, faithful, soldiers, parishioners, of individuals under his jurisdiction . . . . The head is not above the law, or if he is, it is because he is and must be more obedient than the others. He has a daily acquaintance with how difficult obedience is when it is incumbent on him to obey the form which the common good presents itself to him every day. He also knows the painfulness of obedience when he, too, is crushed by an incident which unveils to him, as it did to Abraham, an even higher

99

good which is the sole Will of God, given without commentary.

All this gives us to understand that we do not grasp authority in the least when we continue to look upon it after the fashion of pagans — man's right over man. Authority is another kind of service that man renders to man, another facet of obedience. "Master and servant," Hegel said, "are the basis of dialectics and of the movement of history!" And Marx added: "Here is the fatal source of conflict and of the constant struggle for renewal."

Certainly, this is true, O hard prophets, if master and servant fulfill each other, as Pascal would have said "in different subjects"; if he who is master is different, if he who is servant is different. But the example of him who said that he did not come to be served but *to serve* teaches us that we are all masters and servants to some degree; furthermore he teaches us that the more we are masters the more we ought to have the spirit of servants. There are no dialectics here, but instead the divine paradox of the gospel.

24 *Growing Old Together*

LET US now proceed to the third phase of love's growth: old age. Is love still possible at this time of life? Is it not transformed into something entirely different?

Love at this third stage is a continuation of the love of the two preceding stages. Only here it is perfected. It is not a metamorphosis but an Assumption. At this point we often note a symbiosis between the two partners; with age, the traces of sex are less apparent on their faces, and because of a kind of mimesis and consent, husband and wife almost begin to resemble each other. Just as autumn leaves of different species resemble one another more closely than do those of spring (the veins are alike when the sap is used up), so likewise in old age the resemblance between the wife and her own mother is intensified.

Grand-paternity and grand-maternity differ greatly from the first. Perhaps there has not been sufficient stress on this point, which is obscured by the apparent near-identity between the words father and grandfather, mother and grandmother. Paternity has for its object the being who is the issue of your blood and the work of your love. It is immediate; it is carnal; it is rather limited.

Grand-paternity is of an entirely different nature, for the grandson owes nothing to the works of his grandfather who did not conceive him any more than the grandmother has begotten him. In appearance the grandson is farther removed than the son: he is the son of a stranger. But the grandfather's love for him does not spring from mere affinity. This child, while having his own blood, also has someone else's: there are four ancestors in him. And by clinging to this virtual being (all the more so since he will probably not live to see him mature) the grandfather's love detaches itself, extends itself, sublimates itself. He loves less severely, less proudly.

The shortness of the ensuing days, the idea that after all, life is very brief, that childhood is the age that we ought to enjoy most, the memories of the first childhood that become so keen with the onslaught of old age, the desire also of leaving behind a sweeter image of oneself than one bequeathed to one's own children — always a little too harsh because of our severities — everything tends to compel the grandfather to be the image of Goodness itself. All that remains for him to do is to draw up his will, that is, to testify as to what he wanted to accomplish and what he could not accomplish, leaving to others the task of carrying on and of drawing up another testament. This state of indifference and of light is favorable to love, at least to the love of complacency, of peace and of oblation which is the final stage of all love.

In this horizon, married love can be reborn under an unknown form. We never hear of old people getting divorced. Generally speaking, they have a physical need of each other's presence. Old age brings the couple even closer together. One necessarily finds the bond stronger than before because of the remoteness of the children, so frequent in our personalist civilization, because of infirmities which force us to lean on the support of the other, because of the quasi-animal habit of being together. In this third state, love is divested of passion, it is not even, properly speaking, a sentiment; it takes on some-

thing sacred — I am tempted to say, *sacral* — because of the time which has elapsed. Maturity having finally taken place, new increase is impossible. The approach of the end gives it a character of immobility. Love repeats itself, it finds itself, it remembers itself. Nothing can excite it, but neither can anything subdue it. It is beyond fluctuation and almost outside of time already.

At this stage love bears a resemblance to religion. To the eyes of those who see it from the outside, the couple has become a priest — a priest of primitive religion, the religion of fire, the religion of the home. It is true that for love to reach such heights, for it not to be a solitary sacrifice, death must intervene. This is the moment to establish the relationship between love and death: it is fundamental, since love is a means invented by nature to conquer death.

25 *Love, the Conqueror of Death*

IN THE ordinary course of life, the thought of death does not have a salutary effect. It is veiled by the social lie, mutual illusion, a religious silence. Every time a mortal threat hangs over a couple (as happened formerly with almost every birth), love becomes concentrated; a union in which one of the partners has not run the risk of death would not have any deep-rooted strength. Following the death of a child, the love of the spouses is again steeped in its origins, being sanctified by a permanent and silent sorrow. (Some time ago I read some admirable thoughts on the subject of this rebirth of love by Jacques Madaule, but I have forgotten where.) But love must measure up to death one last time.

Generally, the husband is the first to leave. To this idea custom has added that the man be the older partner. Woman is made to weep over man and not vice versa. For love to become a cult, death is required. Once it has done its work, a destiny is brought to an end at once. The life of the deceased then looms up with the beauty of a work of art, to which only meanings and symbols can be added; it is complete unchangeable. Just as we cannot fully appreciate anything until it is past, so after the death of one spouse the survivor comes to a full realization of the other's love. This mechanism is at work during simple separation, which is a metaphorical death; but the fact that the spouse will return spoils the effectiveness of the absence. When the absence becomes definitive, all history becomes legend. All we remember of the deceased is *what should be said,* what is noble, what deserves being told. We no longer remember the daily annoyances, the domestic manias, the family quarrels, the cutting words. We evoke the oldest memories, sometimes the most fabricated ones. This does not mean that they are the most false ones, because the truth of a man lies not in his moods, nor is the history of man found in his daily life. The image my wife will keep of me — that of a good, courageous and sacrificing lover — is not my real image. What she will remember is my ideal self, the one I strove for, the one I wanted to have preserved, the one that must be remembered by those who survive me. This explains why the dead are more beautiful than the living.

Just as a child's memory of his father is riddled with regrets and remorse for his belated understanding of him, so the image a widow retains is more real than the tangled impression of her husband she had during their life together. In the absence of a sensible support, in the impossibility henceforth of caring for and being concerned for the other, of receiving a response, love reaches the heights of sacrifice. Around a tombstone, before unimaginable remains, the mind recreates an almost divine image. For some, this separation of the body is the hardest thing of all in the life of love: if the essence of love consists in constant communication, then we can understand how absolute absence is unbearable. But alas! Time makes everything bearable, even the impossible.

Here, too, nature has provided mechanisms of compensation. Physical contact effects more than fecundity. It also brings about an impregnation: that all the elements of our substance penetrate each other and run over into another humanity. Naturally the impregnation of bodies is but the support of a psychological, moral, even mystic impregnation. Hence the impression (and perhaps the reality) of a dwelling of the one in the other which is not broken by absence and which can be all the more keen the more physical life slackens, the closer we come to port. In his poem of the love of old people, entitled *Booz Endormi,* Victor Hugo makes Booz say:

> How long it has been since she with whom I slept,
> O Lord, left my couch for yours;
> Our beings still commingle and are twin,
> She half alive and I, half dead.

26 Shall We See Each Other Again?

CHRISTIANITY gives no precise answer to this question. It teaches the immortality of the soul, or rather the resurrection of the complete person but not the eternity of the couple, because it respects the impenetrable. Yet a couple (if it has spent its temporal life perfecting its bonds) seems more indestructible than the isolated soul. On the other hand, can the being of one, immortal without the other, find its happiness far from the other? Even if the other is a great sinner?

The Catholic religion is full of shadows and restraint regarding the states after death, most likely because from the beginning it had to resist the need of imagining the world beyond the grave as a continuation of life on earth. But it seems difficult to imagine that human love should be foreign to life after death. To conceive the permance of *me* without the permanence of *us* seems difficult, unless we assume metamorphoses, substitutions of being which will end in taking our personality from us. If God is essentially love, if likewise his infinite life is a gift, it is unthinkable that God should extinguish in us forever our ability to love, which is our closest resemblance to him. Here we come up against the extremely difficult question of the persistence of time in eternity.

SHALL WE SEE EACH OTHER AGAIN?

It is inconceivable that time *as such* exists in eternity without making eternity temporal. But it is difficult to think that eternity absorbs in itself the complete essence of time. We cannot admit that the love of the couple subsists in the great beyond under its earthly form, even if it were sublimated; would that not be the definition of torture, such as Dante suggested for Francesca da Rimini? On the other hand, the conditions of eternal life need not be so new, so radically different from our own, that they abolish all expression of a deep love, especially if this love consisted in preparing for life eternal through the joys and trials of this life which is so sweet, so hard, so transitory . . . .

In this new and eternal state, love is transformed quite profoundly: those who love each other will henceforth love each other *in God*. And we cannot imagine, conceive, or even understand what it means to love each other, to know each other, to see each other in God. I would say that henceforth God plays on our instrument. God alone holds the bow: human beings are strictly sonorous chords. If the couple subsists in a sublime way, they do so only to enter with the great throng of the saints into the circuit of eternal love.

27 *The Incommunicable*

OFTEN, when we have lost one of our own and when we realize that it is now impossible to talk with him, we reproach ourselves for having "let him go" without having confided to him our cares, our desires, an undisclosed secret or even our love for him, love that we had hidden during his lifetime either through modesty, through the monotony of our daily life or because it was practically impossible to have such definitive, completely open-hearted talks with a father, a mother or a spouse. Furthermore, we did not know how to talk to him. Does he now know that which we could not, that which we dared not say? Or will he continue to be ignorant of it forever? We are silent regarding such anguishes that mount in our souls after separation — and yet what man is not aware of them?

But can we or rather should we tell everything to each other during life? Are there in one's ordinary life such things as tranquil, regal moments when a conscience can unburden itself to another conscience to the extent that no corner is left unveiled, that there is no desire to say more? I do not think so. I often observed that when a thought weighs heavily on us and must be voiced, we go away with the idea that we have not made ourselves understood, that what was essential was not clearly stated, that much more remains to be said, perhaps everything. This is all the more so if it is a question of a particular sentiment. What makes us think that a deep love can be expressed in a letter or even in hundreds of letters, in a word or even in thousands of words?

This should not surprise us. This margin of the inexpressible, which is the environs of our most intimate thoughts, comes from their deep-rootedness. We must not seek to limit it, but must accept it as a necessary obscurity, like that *sfumata* that Leonardo da Vinci substituted for contours and which was, so he said, his last difficult work. . . .

Sleep in peace, my well-beloved dead; listen to me from your mysterious abode! From now on you will know all that I cannot express about myself. And if I seemed to you to be distracted, if I left some of your questions unanswered, if even I concealed a part of my person from you (not out of malice but through false modesty) be assured now of seeing me clearly, such as I am, and even as I do not realize myself to be.

When those close to each other do not understand each other, is an *explanation* necessary? Yes — if it is straightforward and bears on some points of fact unknown to or ignored by the other and which are the cause of misunderstanding. No — if the explanation gives rise to resentment, to black moods and to those hideous accusations of friend against friend, of son against father . . . .Then self-explanation is equivalent to giving oneself the right to express one's dregs, and dregs give the wrong impression. In evil as in good, we must not coerce the incommunicable.

The rules of politeness apply here. They oblige us to communicate ordinary and proper sentiments in a measured and suitable amount. It is the same with prayer. The unspeakable groaning of the Spirit have no use in the assembly of God's people, and liturgical forms substitute prayers for them in which each one can understand what the other has said because it is the fixed and traditional prayer of all.

What is incommunicable in us belongs to God. It must be left to him.

28   *From Eve to Mary*

THE Bible (that book where each being is described under his eternal type) has left us two profiles of womanhood: Eve and Mary. Eve stands at the origin of things, at the beginning of the first covenant; Mary stands at the axis of history, when the second and eternal convenant between God and man was established. And both these two types of womanhood reflect a ray of light which gives her some insight into the mystery of woman.

Eve was vulnerable. She was gracious but frail. She was seduced and she seduced in turn. She was coquettish: she prated even with the devil. She ended in resembling the devil and in becoming for Adam the image of temptation. She did not go straight to the point; we would say that she beat around the bush. She obtained Adam's consent, charm giving to evil the exquisite appearance of good. She was out of step with reality; only after the fall did she realize that she was naked.

But Eve also had her greatnesses of which Milton and Peguy sang. She was a fountainhead. Although she lost her innocence, she kept the freshness of primeval creation. She symbolizes incertitude and the promise of those beings who

113

originate. After the fall, she was courageous in the face of suffering. She braved the formless mass of feminine pain. We surmise that she was proud, tough, unconcerned about cares, very generous.

We do not picture her without Adam, from whom she was separated neither in good, in the fall, nor in expiation. We never see one without the other. She was taken from the side of man during his ecstatic sleep: she was his dream incarnate. If he sinned, he did so, as Duns Scotus said, because he loved her too much. The Bible does not reproach them too severely: it rather excuses this inexperienced young couple. In frequent rereading of this story, I have always found an accent of pity, of the Creator's pity for this first woman made of flesh and of frailness, who could not resist the suggestion of the devil.

Mary is the other face of woman, the one that is turned both toward the heights and the depths. Purity in her not only means absence of taint, but simplicity: the simplicity of white light that stores up within itself all the colors of the spectrum. Purity is condensation carried to the extreme. We dare not say that Mary was beautiful, if by beauty we mean splendor of form; for those persons she has appeared to in visions, she seems have had a beauty of irradiation. But there is something deeper than beauty. It is the presence of a soul in the lines of a face, in its gaze, in its way of smiling: a kind of abandon, as if there were goodness in the heart of beauty. It is grace. Mary is grace. Over and above pleasure, there is happiness; more than happiness there is joy. Mary is the cause of joy.

Woman is twofold: she has the power to drag a man down to stupidity, to weakness, to foolishness; but she can also make him attain, for love of her, to excellence. A woman can even teach a man to forego the pleasures she gives him. A woman's presence lends sweetness to sacrifice; she can make death bearable when he dies in her arms. For believing humanity, Mary was the one who made labor delightful. Think of the cathedrals, a work accomplished by superhuman effort, those massive structures pierced with light, which veneration to Mary made possible.

In Mary there is also the source of courage, which is will grasped at its source in the moment when we say "yes." This is so true that the first gospel quote of her is the word "yes" — "Be it done to me according to thy word" (Lk. 1, 38). This consent given prior to all that can supervene in the register of misery and grandeur (for we know that all will come to pass, and following the excess of evil, perhaps even the excess of good and happiness?), this "yes" spoken by a woman to the Child as yet sexless, without a face, whom she awaits in her body and who will be for her a burden, a concern, mystery and glory — such is the word that every woman pronounces, so to speak, at every moment.

Finally, in Mary, there is furthermore the immobility of acceptance, the erect posture she maintained in the face of sorrow. And that is why she is often represented standing before the second tree, the Tree of the Cross which corresponds to the tree of the forbidden fruit; Mary carries on the combat where Eve yielded. But, at Christmas, painters prefer to picture her kneeling and leaning over the Child. No painter has ever dared imagine the first woman doing just that, yet Genesis calls Eve the mother of all the living.

Eve, who was a mother so many times and the mother of strong men, has not been portrayed as a mother. Yet Mary, the virgin mother of one Person, has in our Western civilization become the type of mothers and their constant image.

The reason is that Eve lacked that spiritual maternity which embraces physical maternity. We cannot imagine Eve as endowed with that fullness of courage which is patience, with that fulness of speech which is silence. She went half-way in everything and that undoubtedly was the root-cause of her fault — not so much having committed evil and spoken the lie as not having gone the whole way of truth and fidelity.

At Christmas, Mary is on her knees in adoration before Origin, this Child who is her Creator and whom she sees under such a humble beginning. She sees the future in this new-born Babe under the form of so frail, so vulnerable a being. We are sure he will suffer a great deal, that he will make others suffer very much; but we also know he will triumph in the end despite everything, and that he will sanctify those who wish it. Mary divines the cross and glory, these two associated signs.

Far more than Eve, Mary is at the beginning of everything; for the true beginning is the rebeginning after a first fall, the second innocence, the moment when we see that the "fault is a happy one" and that everything will be remade on a better plane.

Eve, I repeat, is that enigma of the fault of an instant which endures through its consequences. Mary is the mystery of the pardon that goes on eternally.

Eva. *Ave.* Spell Eva backwards and you have Mary's word, the one the angel used to greet her. The change is a very minor one. The difference very slight. A smile, a slight lengthening of the lips and all is changed. Everything changes meaning with Mary (just as everything changes meaning with a smile). "The presence of the eternal Woman draws us upwards," Goethe said toward the end of the second Faust.

And so perhaps now I can understand the twofold meaning of the word grace, and why men by a sublime confusion have applied the same word to what is most visible in human beauty and what is most hidden in God.